Psychosocial Development of Children

Psychosocial Development of Children

Irene M. Josselyn, M.D.

New York ● JASON ARONSON ● London

Library of Congress Cataloging in Publication Data

Josselyn, Irene Milliken, 1904-1978.
  Psychosocial development of children.

  Includes bibliographical references.
  1. Child psychology. 2. Psychoanalysis.
I. Title.
BF721.J6 1978   155.4'18   78-3112
ISBN 0-87304-154-2

Printed in the United States of America
Designed by Sheila Lynch

Contents

Foreword

When *Psychosocial Development of Children* by Irene M. Josselyn, M.D., was first published by Family Service Association of America in 1948, it provided a new framework for dealing with the practical problems of helping children negotiate the hazards of the growth process; it related psychological factors to social development. The response to its publication was immediate, and over the years it has been reprinted twenty-one times.

Since it was first published, *Psychosocial Development of Children* has become established as a basic guide for the caseworker in understanding the interaction of social and emotional influences on the life of the child. It has also come to be regarded as a true classic in the field.

The continuing interest in the book eventually led to a realization of the need to expand and update the material, and Dr. Josselyn agreed to undertake this important task. This second edition of *Psychosocial Development of Children* retains the basic concepts of the earlier work, but it includes a number of new ideas not previously expressed by the author. The book is further enhanced by the avoidance of unnecessary jargon and presentation of the material in a clear and factual manner. In summary, Dr. Josselyn has, in this second edition, espoused her belief in the conditions essential for ensuring the maximum physical, mental, and emotional development of the child, as changing sexual, intellectual, and constitutional needs make themselves known at different age levels.

Dr. Josselyn died before publication of this second edition was completed. However, the usefulness of this book and the validity of her ideas live on as a fitting memorial to a talented and creative woman.

Jacqueline Marx Atkins
Director, Publications Service
Family Service Association of America

Preface

This book is a revision of my previous book on psychosocial development of the child, first published by Family Service Association of America in 1948. Certain concepts that were not present in the original book are now introduced. It is, on the whole, based on psychoanalytic concepts although many ideas, such as those discussed in the chapter on inherent needs, are the result of case studies.

It may seem rather arrogant to presume that Freud's concept and writings could be reworded more clearly and that ideas could be introduced that were not part of his formulations. However, anyone who reads Freud is impressed by his willingness to contradict a previous formulation that he made. Some of the most creative thinkers in the psychoanalytic group in this country were students of Freud and have introduced ideas that seem alien to his.

The study of human psychology is a complex one. Undoubtedly, any individual whose psychological structure is being scrutinized should be approached with a critical mind and not be placed in a stereotyped formulation. Each individual is a research material in himself and, therefore, a study of that individual should result in some enrichment of thinking in the field of psychology.

Ideas that are introduced in this book are, in part, the result of studying people whose psychological makeup does not seem to fit the classical formulation.

Irene Josselyn, M.D.
Phoenix, Arizona

Environment
and Cultural Milieu

THE ENVIRONMENT and cultural milieu in which a child is reared and which has bearing on the response patterns of the individual in adulthood has several facets. It has a general one to which all children in a relatively homogeneous group are exposed. It has a specific one to which only the individual child is exposed. And it has one in which certain common denominators exist because of the more general milieu, but in which specific differences occur because of the child's place in the milieu.

There are certain inherent drives and maturational stages of development that can be identified as part of the human psychological potential and ultimate configuration. The fate of these inherent drives and the patterns of adaptation established during the maturational stages of development are determined by four broad phenomena: (1) the nature of the cultural milieu into which the child is born; (2) the unique parental response to the child and his behavior; (3) the nature of the inherent drives; and (4) the intensity of those drives. Later chapters elaborate on the latter three phenomena.

The following few paragraphs may seem self-evident, a discourse that has no place in a book discussing normal growth. They are inserted, however, because of the author's experience that most clinicians tend to consider "normal" that which is normal in their own experience and to see as "abnormal" any behavior that does not fit into their definition of normal, irrespective of a different background. Consequently, they are not aware of nor do they seek to become enlightened concerning the broad aspects of the environment to which the child and his parents are adapting. Psychoanalysts are progressively becoming aware that some of Freud's formulations were based on universal psychological components, but that the conclusions drawn were valid only in a Victorian type of culture. Perhaps one of the more striking examples as far as child development is concerned is the concept of latency, a period originally defined as one of "sexual latency." As a result of modern patterns of greater sexual freedom and less repression of sexual curiosity, the latency period is no longer characterized by complete sexual latency. In addition, this period has come to be recognized as an active time of psychological development. Complete sexual repression does not occur, as was postulated in the original formulation, even though there is no new discernible erogenous zone. Psychological growth during this so-called latency period, however, is extremely significant.

The author had a revealing experience concerning the importance of cultural factors during a consultation with a social agency regarding the case of an American Indian woman who was an unmarried mother. This young woman had been reared in a close-knit family in which the tribal standards had been maintained. As a result of her ability and ambitions, and the interest of federal Indian Affairs officers in her superior intelligence, she had been provided a college education leading to professional skills which enabled her to establish a place for herself in the more "civilized" world beyond the reservation. The father of her child was a man from her own tribe. Any attempt on the part of the social worker to have her accept modern medical care, marriage to the father of the child, or adoption for the unborn child met with an alarming unresponsiveness. A description of the woman's behavior clearly fitted the psychiatric classification, schizophrenia. The diagnostic question was why an individual who previously had shown no clear schizophrenic prodromal symptoms had become schizophrenic under the pressure of the social problems besetting an unmarried mother. A discussion with a person who, through careful study, knew the folklore of this particular tribe cleared up the matter. In the tribe, pregnancy without marriage rites was acceptable if the tribe and not the man were considered the father of the child. At birth, the child became the child of the tribe, not of the real parents, and as such held a unique role in the tribal structure. Every attempt to help this woman according to nontribal customs created conflict for her. She would deprive her child of its true heritage if she accepted any of the superficially easier solutions of her adopted culture. Only when the social worker was able to understand this cultural requirement and reveal her understanding to the woman did the pseudo-schizophrenic picture evaporate. Then the woman was able to discuss realistically the problems with which she was struggling. Previously, she had not been able to fully explain the problem, both because she felt that her worker would not understand and because of the natural reticence of her Indian personality.

The cultural milieu has both a direct and an indirect effect. Whereas individual parents will respond differently to a child's behavior, a difference based upon their tolerance threshold and their specific goals for the child, there are certain general goals in child rearing that are culturally determined. To a greater or lesser extent, parents accept these goals in accordance with their own adaptive patterns. The initial impact of the culture upon the child is indirect; it is transmitted to the child by parental expectations and prohibitions and by parental behavior, which the child gradually imitates. These expectations, prohibitions, and patterns of behavior are determined by cultural patterns. In this way the roots of a cultural heritage pass from parent to child. Later, the influence of the culture on the child's development is more direct, and the child responds to the expectations, prohibitions, and behavior patterns of those in his broader social milieu. As a result, he ultimately contributes to the continuation of the culture by transmitting his heritage to his offspring.

The profound meaning of the cultural heritage is readily recognized in the fate of the individual child who is a member of a primitive tribe or any static cultural group. The many valuable studies by social anthropologists oriented to modern psychological concepts have proven very enlightening in terms of revealing the universality of certain human psychological entities. Studies have also revealed the great variety of manifestations of psychological entities when the environment rigidly defines the accepted modes of their expression.

As cultures become less primitive and more superficially similar, there is a tendency to assume that the similarities overrule the dissimilarities, and a homogeneity is fallaciously taken for granted. The child reared in an environment that is structured in part by the teachings of Catholicism will inherit certain patterns that are significantly different from those of a child reared in a primarily Protestant, Orthodox Jewish, or Moslem milieu. The child reared in an environment in which his own father is considered the powerful authority to whom all others are subject will be adapting to and acquiring patterns quite different from those of the child reared in a culture in which father and mother are equally authoritarian, in which the mother is more so, or in which both parents are subject to the control of the senior members of the family unit. A child who is a member of a national group in which dictatorship is the accepted form of government has a very different cultural heritage from that of a child reared in a democracy, a limited monarchy, or a nation constantly torn by revolt. Thus, he will utilize different modes of adaptation in the process of healthy psychological development and can be expected to evolve a personality suitable to his milieu. What may be a healthy adaptation in one cultural milieu may be a neurosis if it occurs in an individual in another. It is important not to confuse one's psychological concepts with one's sociological and political beliefs.

Modern psychology has been criticized because of the faulty assumption that its teaching implies that the psychologically healthy individual is that hypothetical person who has been reared in an environment that has permitted the free expression of all primitive impulses and therefore who has no personality or character patterns determined by his relatedness to others. The modern psychological theory of personality development is based upon a study of people, not on the basis of wishful thinking. Just as this was true of the behaviorist school, as exemplified by John B. Watson,[1] it is equally true of the followers of Freud, as well as those who, with or without Freudian psychological orientation, are studying the development of human responses and their modification during the growth process in individuals. What an individual does is subjected to scrutiny, then an attempt is made to understand why he does it. This no more implies condemnation of the behavior or criticism of its causation than—to use another specialty of medical science—does the biochemist's study of the human body's reaction to bacteria imply condemnation of the sore throat that streptococci cause or condemnation of the throat that becomes sore. Other bacteria promote health and they are also studied. Many psychological responses also promote health.

Observation of human behavior in the attempt to understand it is the basic learning tool of psychology just as the study of bacteria is basic for the biochemist. The reason for understanding the streptococci, so far as human morbidity and mortality are concerned, is to translate that knowledge into the prevention and cure of streptococcic infections. It is also important to understand the normal bacterial flora that provide health so that they will not be destroyed. For the clinician whose work is primarily in the area of psychological health and illness, the reason for studying human psychological responses is also to determine what factors are health promoting and what factors are disease promoting—the former to be strengthened, the latter to be eradicated or their effectiveness curbed.

1. John B. Watson, *Behaviorism* (New York: W. W. Norton and Co., 1958).

Physical health, although in itself a complicated concept, is today, at least, easier to define and foster than psychological health. As general and as frustratingly intangible as it is, perhaps the clearest conceptualization that can be offered at present in regard to psychological or mental health is that of a state of functioning through which the optimum gratification of the individual's inherent needs and the optimum expression of his internal urges are provided through the resources and outlets available in the environment, and those resources and outlets are utilized in a fashion that contributes to the enrichment of that environment. It is perhaps not unnecessarily redundant, however, to remind the reader that just as a physically and psychologically healthy person is not necessarily a person we like, so also is a healthy social structure not necessarily a form we like. It is simply a social structure that is not threatened by morbidity or mortality.

As long as the individual finds optimum gratification for his needs and optimum outlets for his internal impulses within the framework of the social structure, he will be psychologically healthy. As long as the social structure provides optimum gratifications and outlets for the majority of its members, it also will be healthy. The characteristics of the social structure will determine the form of the gratifications and outlets found by the healthy individual. Conformity to a rigid social structure may provide adequate rewards for its members so that mental health is actually fostered by the rigidity—primitive tribal structures, for example, dictate rigidity for tribal members. To the extent that the culture is malleable, it will be modified by the individuals who compose it. Thus, a more malleable social structure gradually changes. It, therefore, offers more choice of gratification and a greater variety of outlets and, in so doing, it broadens the area of potential expression and thus fosters cultural enrichment. At the same time, its very changeability gives less definition to available gratification and outlets and easier access not only to more enriching experiences, but also to ones that prove to lead to the dead end of neurosis and psychosis. A democratically based culture, for example (that is, the most malleable social structure yet known and, therefore, the one offering the most enriching experience for those seeking individuality), also offers the least defined social structure and, therefore, the greatest possibility of channeling needs and urges into a blind alley.

Statistics in regard to the frequency of mental illness in a certain cultural milieu in contrast to its frequency in others are subject, of course, to the errors involved in the diagnostic terminology. It would seem theoretically inevitable, however, that the culture that provides the greatest individual freedom and the fewest predetermined, definitive patterns for adaptation would also tend to have a higher percentage of people who, seeking ways of adaptation to meet their own psychological needs and urges, end up in a nonproductive blind alley. The significant implication is not that a more structured society prevents neurosis and psychosis, but that the more unstructured a society is, the more important it is to determine those conditions that lead the individual not into blind alleys but into even broader vistas, vistas that are available to the individual only in a nonrestrictive culture.

Subcultures are also an important environmental element. The very lack of a firm overall cultural pattern in such countries as the United States results in these subcultures continuing to exert a strong influence on their members. Anthropologists, psychologists, and other social scientists have studied the effects on the individual of membership in such nationality subcultures as Italian American, Irish American, Polish American, and so on. Other nationality based cultural groups, such as Mexican American and Asian American, have been receiving attention in recent years, and there is growing awareness of the uniqueness of other minority group cultures—black and native American in particular—and their own increasing consciousness of their cultural heritage.

There are other subcultural groups not delineated by nationality or by radical characteristics. For example, in spite of the increasing communication between the different areas of the United States, the individual from Texas has a very different background and can be expected to have certain basic responses different from a person reared in New York City. Or, an intelligent boy whose infancy was spent with a nurse, whose childhood was spent in boarding schools and summer camps, and whose adulthood is expected to be provided for by family business or family fortune will develop adaptive patterns quite different from those of the intelligent boy in a metropolitan slum area who is a part of a family unit that is struggling with physical survival, who must work his way through school, and who, as an adult, will start on the bottom rung of the ladder in his climb to success. Both may reach a psychologically healthy adulthood. On the other hand, both may be unable to cope adequately with the conflicts that are inevitable during the process of maturation. In the event both become psychologically healthy individuals in adulthood, it can be anticipated that their final personality structures will be quite dissimilar. And if they fail to achieve such psychologically healthy growth, the points at which distortions in growth occur will be related not only to the reality situation, but also to the effect that the particular reality situation had on their inherent needs and drives. A person may admire or sympathize with one and not the other. If so, such an attitude reflects the person's own value system, which may mirror his own social philosophy but which has no place in the study of individuals in terms of their health or their illness.

[2]

The Parents

WITHOUT QUESTION the most salient force in the young child's physical and psychological environment is the influence of parents. This chapter focuses on the separate but complementary functions of the mother and the father, the skills required of each, and the influence of the parents on the development of the child.

Mothering

The separation of the mother and the child when the infant is born is only a partial one. The neonate remains as dependent on the mother for having many of his physical needs met as he was during intrauterine life. The infant, for reasons of biological survival, and the mother, for psychological reasons, remain a unit. This early mother-child relationship was first labeled "symbiotic" by Margaret S. Mahler to signify a mutually advantageous union of mother and infant.[1]

The infant's biological need for a symbiotic tie to the mother is self-evident. The psychological meaning to the mother is equally important in terms of the role symbiosis plays in establishing her motherliness.

The mother and infant are one during pregnancy, and the mother does not usually conceptualize the intrauterine infant as something separate from herself. In spite of completing the process of giving birth to the child, the mother feels that the newborn is still of her, an extension of herself. Once the initial void following delivery is over, her first response is to give to the infant as if giving to herself. The nucleus of her emotional world is her infant and herself. Other love

---

1. Margaret S. Mahler, "Autism and Symbiosis, Two Extreme Disturbances of Identity," *International Journal of Psychoanalysis* 39 (1958): 77–83.

objects, formerly meaningful, are now primarily insignificant as they relate to this unit. Her husband is not a sexually loved object; he is the person who shared in making the extension of herself possible and who will now help preserve it. Friends, relatives, and other children in the family are now "modifiers" circulating about the mother-child nucleus.

The intensity of this sense of being a nuclear unit is a brief one for the mature woman. Her ability to adapt to reality, the one within herself, modifies it. Her other children are still extensions of herself, although the tie is more tenuous. Her husband has a need for her and a meaning to her. Her love for him as a person, separate from his role as a parent, has not disappeared but has merely been dormant. He again becomes a sexual object. Relationships once shared with friends and relatives are renewed. The mother-infant relationship, however, remains a symbiotic one, and what the mother does for the infant she experiences as if she were doing it for herself. Her love for her self is shared by the infant as a part of herself. That love, expressed in caring for the helpless infant, is a mothering as well as a self-loving pattern.

The symbiotic relationship between infant and mother is later colored by a new growth in both the mother and the child. The child gradually gains a conceptualization of himself as an individual separate from the objects surrounding him, separate from the mother. The psychologically mature woman experiences a parallel change. The child progressively becomes to her an object separate from herself. It is with this shift in the relationship that the biological mother with her pattern of mothering becomes a psychological mother, her behavior pattern that of motherliness. As the infant matures, the mother-infant tie gradually becomes weaker, but it is to be questioned whether it is ever completely broken. Mahler and Bertram J. Gosliner state, "In humans some emotional tie to the mother persists to the grave."[2]

Because of this symbiotic relationship, the response of a mother to each of her children is unique. With each child the experience is repeated and the mother-child relationship that ultimately develops is determined in part during this early symbiotic period. Because of the variety of experiences possible during any period of life, it is not

2. Margaret S. Mahler and Bertram J. Gosliner, "On Symbiotic Child Psychosis," in *Psychoanalytic Study of the Child,* vol. 10 (New York: International Universities Press, 1955) p.196.

surprising that children in the same family differ in many ways and that the mother's response to each of them is also different.

Motherliness

Modification in the symbiotic relationship is the result of the subsequent development of both mother and infant. In spite of the fact that motherliness originates in the early period of the infant's life, it does not develop satisfactorily unless the woman is mature enough psychologically to find gratification in its evolvement. Motherliness depends on the woman's capacity to feel as though she and the child are one and then to distance herself so that she can give to the child that which he needs as a being separate from herself. The mother must have a capacity for object love, as well as for self love. The residual symbiotic relationship enables her to sense the child's needs. Her capacity for object awareness enables her to see the child as an individual separate from herself. Her ability to love enables her to give to the child without demanding something for herself, and her ability to accept love enables her to establish a psychological interflow between herself and the child. This totality in the mother-child relationship is the essence of motherliness.

Some mothers have such immature needs that they cannot share what they receive, even with an extension of themselves, and they arbitrarily amputate the newborn emotionally. The infant is then deprived of a very important part of his infancy. Other immature women find in the symbiotic mother-child relationship a satisfaction that no other relationship has provided, and they are unwilling to relinquish it. Still other mothers are happy during this early period only to find that, as the child becomes an individual, he has little meaning unless he can continue to provide the pleasure formerly experienced in the symbiotic relationship. Thus, the child is solely an instrument for the mother's pleasure.

A brief comment is in order about an increasingly common experience of the mother in the postdelivery period—the postpartum depression. In her own estimation, the woman may view herself less the ideal mother than, during pregnancy, she fantasized she would become. Her depression is not necessarily a neurotic reaction. She may be fatigued by the delivery and overtaxed by returning home too quickly to resume her household and child-caring responsibilities. She has been through labor and has less energy than is usually available to her. Drained by her responsibility for the child, she becomes discouraged and fears that she is not the "perfect" mother she had hoped to be. Motherliness, however, is inherent in the woman closely bound to her grander function, and the depression that follows the fatigue of delivery does not indicate that she is an inadequate mother or that she rejects her child.

The discussion of motherliness is incomplete if it is described only as a direct outgrowth of an actual symbiotic relationship formed with an unborn child and continued through his neonatal life until he becomes a psychologically and biologically separate individual. Let us assume that there is an instinctual urge in the human female that provides the soil in which mothering patterns are nurtured and from which motherliness grows. The occasional example of pseudocyesis in higher animals other than the human species suggests that although the instinctual urge of mothering is usually dormant unless stimulated by pregnancy, under certain conditions it may be stimulated without pregnancy. There is the case of the dog who, after her first heat and at the time her puppies would have been born, tore up the cushions of a chair and made a nest with the stuffing even though the puppies were nonexistent. For neurotic reasons, women also experience false pregnancy. On the other hand, the inherent urge for mothering finds expression through relationships to helpless beings even though pregnancy is not being experienced. These are not neurotic responses. They are often observed among teachers, nursemaids, single friends of a family, and others, and include people who are "good with small children"; their skill is motherliness—the ability to react by mothering.

There is another aspect to the capacity of women to experience mothering emotionally and to become capable of motherliness. The pattern of expression of internal urges is determined in part through identification with a loved person. The identification with primary love objects is most important for the ultimate personality. A woman who has not experienced mothering or motherliness from her own mother has not only been deprived of an essential gratification in her infancy, she has also been deprived of a primary love object with whom to identify as a mother. Thus, a woman who has lacked an adequate experience with an affective mother person will have more difficulty in channeling her inherent impulses into outlets provided by the mother role. Theoretically, at least, the woman who has not had an adequate mother figure with whom to identify, and who is unable to respond as a mother to her child, is not necessarily an immature person. Rather, she is a person whose discharge patterns are different from those of a woman who has discharge channels available through her identification with an adequate mother person. Women who lacked adequate mothers with whom to identify, however, do sometimes become very adequate mothers. This fact suggests that they found someone with whom they could identify in fantasy, through literature or through other contacts. On the other hand, regardless of the experience of being adequately mothered, it would appear that there is an inherent drive in women toward mothering and motherliness that finds channels for expression in the process of maturation.

Fathering

When question is raised concerning the man's inherent capacity for fathering and fatherliness, an argument usually ensues. Manifestly, there seems to be an inherent capacity in the woman for mothering and for motherliness as there is in females of other animal species. Where men are concerned, however, there is no comparable prototype in other male animals, although in a few species the male has an important role in the care of the young.

If one assumes that the role of father is not inherent in the human species, it would appear that some other component of an instinctual response must be present that explains the protective role men have played since the time of the caveman. Even before social mores frowned upon such behavior, the human male did not abandon the mother and her young. The protective structure may have been of a group rather than an individual nature, but it did exist. Were this not true, the species would probably have become extinct because of the long period of helplessness of the human infant. Under dangerous conditions, the infant would have demanded the mother's protection for too long.

Men have played an important role in the survival of the infant since the beginning of recorded history. Except in cultures in which the role was reversed, the primitive father protected his family by being a warrior and hunter. The protective impulse expressed itself in aggressive activity rather than in direct contact with the infant. Both mother and father, however, perform a protective function. The father protects the mother and child from the threats existing beyond their intimate circle and provides that which enables the mother to carry on her function. The mother protects the infant through intimate contact with him.

Tenderness in a man is acceptable in current Western cultures if it is not too obvious and is masked by roughness or embarrassment, a professional manner (of the physician, for example), or the demands of reality. Both men and women are usually bisexual in nature, yet tenderness is believed to be a feminine quality, and many men are shy about expressing it. They fear that to express the feminine side of their nature openly would lead them to behave in a way that others would consider as "unmasculine."

There is a postnatally determined psychological explanation for tenderness in men. The infant's first identification is with the child-care person. The male infant's first identification, therefore, is with a person of the opposite sex. Thus, one of the major steps in his development must be a shift in identification from the mother to a male figure. In describing the infant's relationship with the mother, Freud states "It is unique without parallel, laid down unalterably for a whole lifetime as the first and strongest love object and as a prototype for all later love relationships for both sexes."[3] Tenderness may have its roots in this early identification and in the residual love that remains a part of both male and female psychology. Whether tenderness is an overlay of an inherent response or an outcome of the early infant-mother relationship, the residual love for the mother suggests a reason for the embarrassment over undisguised tenderness in men. After all, their goal for themselves and the mature woman's goal for them is an adequate identification with masculinity. A residual response, irrespective of its desirability, which has its origin in a feminine identification would be uncomfortable.

Regardless of its origin, tenderness appears to be a potential of the human species of both sexes, a quality to be expressed according to patterns inherent in the sexual differentiation which is, in part, culturally colored. When necessity or social or individual philosophy encourages the man to be fatherly, if he is sufficiently mature he appears to have a real capacity to do so. He can comfortably express tenderness and protectiveness, which are both components of mature love, regardless of their origin.

The preceding section stressed the significance of pregnancy and the infant's neonatal period for the development of mothering and motherliness in the woman. There is a parallel development in the man. During his wife's pregnancy, the soon-to-be-born infant is not an individual organism; it is, as it is to the woman, a part of her. The

3. Sigmund Freud, *An Outline of Psychoanalysis* (New York: W. W. Norton, 1949).

man, if he is sufficiently emotionally mature, responds to the psychological needs of his wife by giving to her and, in so doing, he is also giving to a part of himself—the fetus. He has an advantage over primitive man because he knows his procreative role and accepts it in the beginning of this new life. As the time for the birth of the child approaches, he can tolerate the sexual frustration involved because of his increasing emotional investment in the future child and his tenderness toward his wife.

Fatherliness

The birth of the child typically creates a transient effect in the man similar to that which occurs in the woman. Once he has seen the baby and has "passed out the cigars," his concern is primarily for his wife and his own need for sleep. From that time until the child becomes a person separate from the mother, his psychological response is not dissimilar to hers. He may enjoy holding and caring for the baby not because it is a person, but because it is a part of him and of her. He enjoys providing for his wife's needs if they are maturely expressed. In doing so, he not only expresses his love for her, but also finds an expression for his feeling for her as part of the infant-mother unit. In a sense, he also has a symbiotic relationship with the child; he has developed his ability to be fatherly.

From this interrelationship of father-mother-child the family is born. It is a psychological phenomenon, one of the psychological phenomena that differentiates the highest animal—man—from those of the lower species.

As a child becomes an individual separate from the objects external to him, the father's attitude, as well as the mother's, undergoes a change. He responds to the child with a masculine instead of a feminine mode of expression. His relatedness to the child is dependent upon the same capacities as those important in a woman. Fatherliness becomes a part of his psychological capacity for an emotional interrelationship with his child. Sometimes a father will verbalize this shift of fathering to fatherliness. He will state frankly that he never had any real feeling toward the infant until the baby "began to develop a personality." His wife, recalling his tender interest and care of the infant during the past, cannot believe this is true. She is not aware that she actually has had the same experience. For her, the earlier period was a more vividly charged emotional one.

It therefore appeared more closely linked to a growing interest in the child as a person.

The psychological growth of the man during his wife's pregnancy and the neonatal period of the child's life takes place on a deeper stratum than the obvious aspects of his everyday living. This is also true of the change in the woman. The overlay which is often more apparent is the man's disturbance over loss of sleep, the untidy home, the unwashed diapers, and the interruption of normal routines created by the feeding schedule. These irritating realities instigate responses that appear to disprove any fathering capacity in the man. Sometimes the same difficulties, and her response to them, suggests that the woman's mothering capacity is also a wishful dream of one trying to find something to value in the human species. The proof that it exists in both parents is in the response not to current daily irritations but to major threats to the family. Then the real meaning of the child in the family unit is revealed.

For many reasons, the response of fathering in the man and its growth into fatherliness is a more difficult step in psychological maturation for him than is the parallel development in the woman. The response of others makes it awkward. Men who are to be fathers are more teased than protected, although the reverse is true with women. One wonders whether this teasing is not because of a universal self-consciousness about the inherent tender, protective feelings being revealed by men. A man's role is to provide for his family, and the demands of that responsibility occupy his thoughts to a great extent. During pregnancy, as a woman meets her daily responsibilities she usually thinks less, for example, about the peculiarities of the stock market than about the future child. It is probable that if one made a study of those novels in which the anticipation of the father concerning the birth of the child is described, it would be found that novels concerning men who are manually employed more often stress the dream state of the future father. There are exceptions, of course, but those which deal with men in the business or professional worlds are more apt to stress the future father's preoccupation with his work for the sake of the family. They emphasize the development of domestic crises: The future mother feels that her husband is not really sharing her pregnancy, and the husband feels unable to assure her of his real interest.

Perhaps more significant than either of these external factors are the biological ones. The man protects the child through his care of his wife during the nine months of pregnancy. His function with the infant during the neonatal period is also more remote. He holds the infant at bottle-feeding time, he may change the infant's diapers, but such events are looked on as either privileges or obligations. The mother experiences these things as her "reason for being"; the father's reason for being is less intimately related to the care of the infant. He must do as his ancestors did—go out and hunt for sustenance for his family.

Immaturity in men results in an inadequacy as a father that parallels that of women in accepting their maternal role. In addition, in some instances there is a sense of displacement. Because the man does not share his wife's investment in the child, he may feel excluded. As a result, in anger or discouragement, he either attempts to compete with the child or withdraws from the relationship with both the mother and the child. Actually, competition with the child may occur when either the father or the mother is emotionally immature. An immature woman may resent the father's investment in the child and may try either to minimize the contact between the father and the child or, in resentment, to withdraw emotionally from the child.

Parental Effects on Child Development

The emotional configuration of the parents is of major importance in the psychological development of their offspring. Parents are inevitably the product of their own childhood; their responses to life's demands and gratifications are determined by their own past experiences. A still-current attitude toward parents is that they are the *cause* of psychological problems in their children—an implied or direct censorship of parents for what they have done, although often without knowledge or intention. It appears well established that many of the psychological problems of an individual can be traced to parental behavior and the nature of the childhood response to that behavior. Neither the parents nor the child, however, are to be blamed. The goal of studying this interrelationship and its consequences is to understand, not to condone or condemn, and on the basis of that understanding to explore the possibilities of corrective measures. If blame for the psychological ills of mankind must be placed somewhere, it must be assigned to our human origins, symbolized by Adam and Eve, not to current parents.

A popular cliché today is that an unwanted child is a child doomed to psychological storms which he must either survive by heroic self-struggle with a crippling neurosis or succumb to and be crippled by another type of neurosis; the wanted child has a path of roses already strewn for him. This notion ignores many points. In the biological sense, there is no such person as an "unwanted" child. Biologically, a sperm and ovum meet and are compatible. The result of that meeting is a "wanted" child. Psychologically the problem of whether a child is wanted is extremely complex. Many children whose parents consciously do not want them are, in actuality, unconsciously more longed for than some children whose parents consciously want them. Furthermore, many children are wanted for reasons that, rather than providing them with a future path of roses, will provide a path mostly of thorns. Moreover, it is often not the motivation for parenthood that determines the effectiveness with which the individual assumes the parental role, but rather the capacity the individual has to express that motivation maturely so as to provide the most positive experience for the child.

One of the basic reasons involved in the wish for a child is the refinement of a characteristic of all living organisms: the biological pattern of reproduction. With the complexities of the human species, this biological pattern becomes a conscious wish, subject to the conscious and unconscious reinforcements and inhibitions to which all human wishes are subject. This urge to reproduce is accompanied by an urge to protect that which has been brought to life. The more immature the living organism is at birth, the more carefully and the longer the parent protects it. This protectiveness of the offspring in human beings becomes part of the human psychological format, a configuration with many other facets. It does not terminate when the biological need for protection is no longer necessary but remains a part of the relatedness to the offspring, continuing through the life of the parent and child.

From this protective response, irrespective of the other components, comes the overprotective parent who consciously fences the child in to protect him from dangers. In so doing, the parent deprives the child of an opportunity to grow through the stimulation of exposure to those vicissitudes of life which he is quite capable of mastering. In contrast, however, parental protectiveness wisely geared to the child's capacity for protecting himself is not only an essential need of the small infant, but throughout childhood provides him with the security that enables him to utilize his growing abilities without being exposed to more than he can handle or, if he is, with the assurance that he can turn to his parents for aid and comfort.

From a positive experience with a wisely protective parent an individual develops more mature patterns. It is the capacity of mature individuals to be protective when protection is sought and needed that provides one of the important components of interpersonal relationships. Even a mature individual at times needs and seeks the protection of others. It is not the protective response of parents that serves the child ill or well; it is how maturely the parents express this protective response that determines its effect.

It can be hypothesized that the biologically determined reproductive urge not only becomes a conscious wish in the human being, but, in addition, its fulfillment gratifies an inherent embellishment of that reproductive urge, the wish to create. Fulfillment of that wish results in pride in the creation. Such pride is not just a socially superimposed reaction. Other higher animals less complex than human beings show responses to their offspring that very closely resemble the response of the human parent to a newborn infant. This pride, however, is less all-encompassing and of shorter duration in other animals and, as a consequence, is both potentially less damaging and potentially less helpful than it is in human beings.

The gratification of a creative urge in the human species is not expressed in a stereotyped way. Certain parents, having created a child, cannot tolerate having that creation evolve into any pattern other than that which they themselves continue to create. They attempt to mold the child into a form alien to the child's inherent potential. Such molding, if effective, results in crippling deformities of the personality. Conversely, parents who respond with pride to their newborn child will continue to watch him with pride, to nurture him physically and emotionally, and to guide wisely the development of the potentials of the child they created. From exposure to this parental pride, their child will gain a feeling of respect for and confidence in himself. Parental pride in a child is not in itself destructive; what the parent values and is proud of determines what effect that pride will have. The child benefits by—to use a psychiatric term—the narcissistic investment of the parent in him if that investment fosters his growth rather than distorts it.

The biological urge of the human parents becomes a conscious wish for continuity of their own life through the life of their child. The child represents immortality for them irrespective of what other beliefs they have concerning life after death. A separated part of the parent's being will continue and will reproduce, thus assuring that a part always survives. Again, the parents may attempt to mold the child's life to a form that will be a continuation of a form of life the parents have had. The result may be unfortunate; on the other hand, the wish for continuity can take the wiser form of making it possible for the child to have the life most suited to him.

There are many other ramifications of the expression of the creative urge and it is worthwhile to discuss a few of them because so often they are the basis for indictment of the parents and may, under other circumstances, be important aspects of a desirable parental role.

In the parents' eyes, the child may resemble a dead or living relative who has been significant to the parent, either negatively or positively. The child is frequently equated in some way with a sibling of the parent. This sibling may have been envied or hated during childhood, either consciously or unconsciously. Such a background for the child-parent relationship does not necessarily lead to problems; however, it can be an unfortunate aspect of parental response if the conscious or unconscious identification of the child with the sibling results in overt expression of the earlier hostility. But rarely is the hostility of a sibling relationship completely unequivocal. The positive feelings for the young brother or sister may have been just as repressed as the hostile feelings, or even more so. Positive feelings may be more mobilized in adult life toward the child than they were toward the sibling. The parent may then respond to the child as if he were the sibling, but with warmth and understanding because of the resurgence of the previously hostility masked positive feelings for the sibling.

In her own childhood a mother may have longed to be a boy, and the birth of a male child may reactivate that envy. Now, as the dominant person, she can attempt to curb any masculinity in her child; the situation gives her an opportunity to destroy that which she may envy. Alternatively, she may try to enjoy vicariously through the child the experience of being masculine and attempt to mold his masculinity into a form which she herself had once desired. Either response, and many others rooted in her envy of the male, will cripple the child's development. On the other hand, the mother who has found a mature solution to her earlier envy can find positively expressed satisfaction in watching the maturation of the male child which she herself could not be, but which she has brought into being and nurtured.

A mother with the childhood problem of male envy will, if she has a female child, have constructive or destructive reactions to the little girl. She may resent a girl child as she resented her own self as a female. She may pseudo-identify with the child and assume that the child hates being a girl as she herself did. She may then foster this real or imaginary resentment, either by accentuating the negative aspects of the role of the female or by encouraging the child to prove that "she is as good as a boy." These are 'the responses of a woman who has found no real solution to her problem. A more mature woman with the same background would have experienced the gratifications inherent in being a woman and would, often without being aware of what she was doing, help her girl child to see the uniqueness of being a girl, to accept the uniqueness of others who are boys, and to set her forth early on the road to mature femininity.

A parent may think he sees a similarity between the child and a relative whose character or personality the parent considers undesirable. This recognition may result in anxiety, hopelessness, or indiscriminate disapproval. On the other hand, the child may have certain characteristics that do resemble those of a relative of whom the parent disapproves, but the parent may be sensitive as to why the relative became what he was. This recognition of similarity may be fortunate for the child. The parent who says, "Jimmy reminds me so much of my brother, he's so sensitive. I can see what my parents did that hurt my brother so and undoubtedly crippled him," may be better prepared to handle the needs of his own child than had he not recognized the similarity.

Many other examples of the parent's identifying the child with a loved, hated, or ambivalently meaningful person of the past could be cited, but the few given here are perhaps sufficient to indicate that it is not the identification per se that is significant but rather what is done with that aspect of the parent's response to the child. If it is the only meaning the child has to the parent, then clearly the child has little chance to become who he really is. The parent will act in the framework of whom the child represents rather than who he is in reality. The parent unable to deal maturely with feelings rooted in the immature feelings of the past will also fail in that regard as a parent. But all individual reactions to other people are based in part on past experience, and a parent may understand a child's response because his own past experiences and his past understanding of the feelings of others enable him to empathize with the child.

Parents characteristically want the child to have what they did not have in their childhood. They want this not only because they long to give tangible expression to their love for the child, but also because they hope to relive vicariously what they hope to be a less stressful life. How else can they formulate what they wish for the child except by evaluating their own past experiences and vicariously enjoying different possibilities for the child? Unless they can experience a substitute kind of enjoyment, what assurance would there be that what they offer the child has any merit? Unless they do enjoy the child's experiences in this way, they can provide those experiences only in a textbook fashion, a sterile source of child-rearing goals. The important consideration is how well they understand the particular child's needs and can, through empathy with the child as he is and as he can potentially become, give him the childhood best suited to him and then unconsciously share that experience. The ability to experience vicariously what another experiences is a component of both understanding and enjoying another person.

It is the parent's limitation in what he can enjoy in this manner, rather than his vicarious enjoyment of his child's experiences, that is a disadvantage to the child. The parent who is too lavish with material gifts because he himself had a materially deprived childhood has a limited capacity to enjoy vicariously the child's experiences. He has lost sight of the pleasure of wanting, anticipating, and valuing, and can see only super-saturation as a source of pleasure, thereby depriving the child of an important experience.

An overindulgent parent is often diagnosed as a "rejecting parent." This evaluation is not only too readily given, it also is a questionable diagnostic category. A parent who really rejects a child is extremely rare, if such exists at all. On occasion the clinician interviews a parent who frankly expresses rejection of the child. The parent may be revealing a very general problem, an inability to deal with the psychological conflict that is created in any immature person by the internal as well as the external demands of parenthood. The parent (statistically, it is more often the mother who verbalizes this attitude) is attempting to avoid facing her own internal conflicts by the conscious rationalization that she cannot tolerate the child. One particular child may be the one she says she rejects. In such instances, it is often because this particular child represents to her someone whom she rejects, or she wishes to have the child serve as a substitute for someone and the child fails to fulfill that role. As one talks to such a parent, however, there are usually hints that the rejection is not as complete as she may wish it to appear.

Most parents categorized as rejecting parents are actually ambiva-lent parents. In their relationship with the child, either their hostility is stronger than their affectionate feelings (the latter feelings being repressed in order to avoid the discomfort created by expressing them), or the hostility is repressed because of the conflict that would be created were it brought into the open to contrast with the affectionate feelings. Both hostility and affection may be expressions of emotionally immature aspects of the personality. Immaturity of emotional response, however, should not be equated with rejection; it may, instead, represent ambivalence. Parents are ambivalent toward their child if for no other reason than that the child sometimes exhausts the most mature parent. Again, it is not the presence of the ambivalence but how that ambivalence affects the child relationship that is important.

In many instances, the behavior of the overprotective or the overpermissive mother reveals her ambivalence by her denial of one phase of it. Her fear that her child will suffer an injury may indicate a deeply unconscious desire that such an injury occur. But her behav-ing in a manner that serves to prevent the fulfillment of her unconscious wish also indicates the degree to which she does not wish the child to be injured. In contrast, some overprotective mothers are revealing a much more all-encompassing insecurity for reasons originating in their own past. They are insecure about their relation-ship with anyone meaningful. This insecurity becomes symbolically expressed by fear of fatal injury to anyone they love.

Overly permissive parents may be so because they unconsciously wish injury to the child and deny this to themselves by their compliance with what they interpret as modern child-rearing meth-ods, permitting the child to bring on his own destruction. They may have an unconscious wish to straitjacket the child and, as with the overprotective parent, deny this hostile impulse by quite opposite behavior. Such parental behavior is ambivalent behavior, not rejec-tion. Other parents are overpermissive because they fear their child will reject them, an insecurity in interpersonal relationships that is a residual of their past.

In summary, capacity for a parental type of emotional response to a child is probably the most psychologically mature response attained by a human adult and is, in all likelihood, only relatively possible for anyone to achieve. Being a parent is not simple; understanding a parent is even more complicated.

[3]

The Neonate

ANY ATTEMPT TO TRACE the steps in human development from birth to maturity brings to light unanswered questions in regard to the significance not only of the intrauterine experience, but also of the very early postnatal period. What is the infant at birth? And what characterizes the postnatal period?

Because of the relative structural immaturity of the neonate, his behavior cannot be evaluated in terms of later psychological constellations. A neonate responds in a way more comparable to that of an unconditioned reflex: in other words, on the basis of an inherent response pattern. In this early period the psyche and soma cannot be differentiated. Edward Glover has referred to this period as the "psychosomatic" period in which is found the "simplest form of psychosomatic reactions: in other words, simple disorders of excitation and discharge. These are without fixed psychic content."[1] He has called this behavior the "primary functional level of development."[2] Margaret S. Mahler, another careful student of early child development, states: "At birth the mental apparatus of the infant is identical with his somatic organization, with only certain reflex reactions indicating affective conditions."[3]

Early Postnatal Response

There are three broad types of infant behavioral responses that are readily discernible in the early postnatal period.

1. A startle reaction to loud noises results in the physical response of

1. Edward Glover, "Functional Aspects of the Mental Apparatus," *Yearbook of Psychoanalysis,* vol. 7 (1951): 90–97.
2. *Ibid.*
3. Margaret S. Mahler, *On Human Symbiosis and the Vicissitudes of Individuation: Infantile Psychosis,* vol. 1 (New York: International Universities Press, 1968), p. 7. The author would modify Mahler's statement by saying "*an anlage* to affective conditions."

forming a fist. Until there is evidence that this response serves some other purpose, it would seem most easily explained as an inherent response serving to alert the individual to danger. Because there is no cortical awareness of the nature of the danger, and because the biological immaturity of the neonate makes it impossible for him to depend on himself, the startle reaction leads neither to further mobilization for defense nor to actions of a defensive character, and the neonate returns to his previous quiescent state.

2. The second type of response is related to body functioning. In his waking hours the neonate does not always lie perfectly quiet. Even though he manifests no signs of physical discomfort, physically he may be quite active within the limits of his neurological control. His arms and legs thrash about in what appears to be purposeless behavior; he attempts to turn his head from side to side. When placed on the abdomen, some newborn infants will lift their heads and, in turtle fashion, seem to observe their environment, although knowledge of the neurological development of the eyes suggests that they see little more than a blur. This muscular activity undoubtedly serves to stimulate the growth of muscle tissue since unused muscles tend to atrophy, but the teleological value of the activity does not fully explain its appearance. It would seem likely that some internal, possibly biochemical, stimulus creates tension which is discharged in motor activity, the response resulting in a sense of relaxation. This is a prepleasure experience. (The author reserves the concept of pleasure to imply a psychological experience.) Motor activity, whether as a means to an end or for its own sake, also remains a source of pleasure for many more mature organisms. As one watches the kicking and arm waving of the slightly older child as he coos and laughs without direct response from others, the gratification that motor activity provides, regardless of why it does so, is clear.

The neonate also shows a physical response to cutaneous stimulation, to rocking movements, to being held, and to changes in position. Margaret A. Ribble found that the heart and respiratory rate in the newborn is more quickly established when he has optimal stimulation of this kind.[4] A distressed type of crying will often ease briefly if the neonate is provided with some such experience. Why this is true is not known; it may be a continuation of comparable experiences of intrauterine life. But, for the neonate, these experiences either

---

4. Margaret A. Ribble, *The Rights of Infants* (New York: Columbia University Press, 1943), pp. 18, 38.

relieve tension or at least bring a state of relaxation that again is a prepleasure experience.

3. The third group of responses are those that are more clearly explained as relating to the survival needs of the infant and again have characteristics of an inherent pattern of response that serves the aim of physical survival. The cardinal example of this response is the infant's sucking reflex which is teleologically recognized as important because of its essential role in survival. But why does a baby suck? There are certain patterns of neonatal behavior that appear to have fundamental significance but for which the stimulation is not yet clear. Within the limits of our present knowledge, it would appear valid to assume that such responses occur in order to reduce tension. Sucking is perhaps the most clearly defined example. Sucking movements occur during intrauterine life. Although it could be postulated that intrauterine sucking is a response to a state of physiological hunger, the sucking does not serve the purpose of alleviating hunger because nutrition is not adequately received in this way, even though some intake of amniotic fluid may be of nutrient value. An observation perhaps of more significance is that certain neonates will continue sucking movements of the mouth even after an adequate intake of food. And if by chance the infant's fist is in contact with his mouth, he will suck it.

There is another observation in regard to the significance of hunger in instituting the neonate's sucking response. Stomach contractions similar to those identified as hunger contractions in the more mature organism occur in the neonate from two to four hours following feeding. These contractions often do not disturb sleep. More significantly, in the more mature organism hunger contractions stop when food is in the mouth. In the neonate, they do not stop until the stomach is partially filled. Moreover, even though the infant at the breast gets a large percentage of his total intake of milk in the first few minutes of sucking, he will continue to suck. Also, if a bottle-fed baby, crying because of "hunger," is given a bottle from which the milk does not flow, he will suck rhythmically and apparently with satisfaction for an appreciable length of time before he responds to the failure to receive nourishment.

These findings in regard to both the sucking behavior associated with hunger and the quieting of the hungry baby before physiological hunger is relieved suggest that the sucking reflex is an inherent response to some stimulus that is activated by a variety of factors, only one of which is hunger. There may be an inherent need to suck, which then serves the biological function of permitting food to enter the mouth.

Although this material is only a superficial and much-abbreviated discussion of neonatal behavior, it is presented to justify a basic but still unanswered question in regard to later psychological development: What is the nature of the prepsychological state in the early postnatal period? Glover discusses this early period in this way: "It is at this stage that individual factors combine with constitutional factors to form a predisposition respectively to the psychosomatic disorders, to the psychoses, and to the psychoneuroses of later life."[5] He describes this stage as "the primary functional level of development, or the psychosomatic stage."[6]

In the neonate, gratification of a need stimulus and thereby the reduction of tension results in the response of the total organism, a total psychosomatic response. In the first few days of life, the typical response of the sucking-feeding neonate when gratified is sleep—at this age, a physiological state. Other stimuli, with the exception of such painful ones as colic, loud noises, or an open diaper pin, are quiescent. René A. Spitz states, "In the first stage the emotional organization varies from excitation to quiescence. In the first stage quiescence appears to be sought and we can perhaps assign this stage to the nirvana principle. It is a stage which appears to be more biologically than psychologically understandable."[7] Glover states, "A primitive phase does not cease to function because it has reached the limits of its expansion and is overlaid by subsequent more organized layers. In contradistinction to the atrophy of certain primitive physiological systems or organs, the earlier mental system continues to function throughout life alongside more developed organizational institution."[8] It is hypothesized by the author that this early response picture does not disappear but becomes amplified. It loses its original discernible identity, but it stilll remains a core of later development.

The Prepsychological Stage of Development

The first level of psychological development is identified as the oral stage. In the study of psychological distortions of growth, this stage

5. Glover, "Functional Aspects of the Mental Apparatus," p. 97.
6. *Ibid.*
7. René A. Spitz, "Relevancy of Direct Infant Observation," in *The Psychoanalytic Study of the Child,* vol. 5 (New York: International Universities Press, 1950), p. 68.
8. Glover, "Functional Aspects of the Mental Apparatus," p. 93.

is often discussed in terms of the oral gratification the infant receives. As will be pointed out in the following chapter, other gratifications of this period are of equal importance. For the purposes of this discussion, however, some difficulties that are attributed to an unsatisfactory oral stage of development may be related instead to the failure to gain a reduction in tension as defined in the primary reflex arc. The inherent response fails to accomplish tension reduction without external help. People continue to take in food when no longer hungry not necessarily because of oral gratification, but for the sole purpose of gratifying a need stimulus that originated in hunger.

From a clinical standpoint, the gratification of a need stimulus would seem to have significance in regard to the early etiological factors in psychosomatic illnesses. According to recent research, certain character types develop certain psychosomatic illnesses under the pressures of certain types of life situations. The foundation of this phenomenon may be found in the early period of neonatal life in which early frustrations leave a biological memory trace, the resulting tension being reactivated later under certain stress situations.

An adult who suffers from obesity that is a result of overindulgence in food is perhaps another example of this same phenomenon. Early in psychoanalytic therapy, the symbolic meaning of food, the function overeating serves, and a variety of other aspects of the problem become apparent. The patient describes a frantic urge to eat which he can deal with not by insight but only by "self-control"—a conscious acceptance of the tension and tolerance for that tension. In the opinion of the author, if this tension is of a biological nature and thus rooted in the problems of the primary level of development, it would explain the difficulty of treating obesity either in childhood or adulthood. Obesity is treatable, with or without insight, only if the patient can find other ways of releasing the tension through a symbolic gratification or can tolerate a "biological" tension. This tension appears to have roots that are not subject to cognitive recognition leading to a type of insight that will enable the individual to reevaluate it and thereby adjust to it on a more mature level. Rather, it appears to have a precognitive origin.

There is no reason to assume that the stimulation and the tension created by that stimulation are of uniform intensity in the individual at different times, or identical in intensity in different individuals. It is also possible that in some instances the stimulus-tension phenomenon can be discharged through other channels than the inherent one. Infants with cleft palates suck even though the sucking is unsatisfactory and nutrition must be obtained by other means. A study of the behavior of somewhat older children with cleft palates indicates that they later exhibit greater motor activity than the average child. Is this the use of a different channel for the tension reduction function of sucking in response to the stimulus for the sucking-tension-sucking-relaxation sequence? A further study of these children could throw light on the eventual fate of the sucking stimulus.

In the neonate, if tension resulting from either internal or external stimulation is not discharged through the reflex arc of the inherent response, massive discharge will occur that has no relationship to the ordinary channels of discharge; for example, the baby cries and thrashes about. Along with this easily discernible discharge of tension, there may also be internal manifestations as seen in colic, diarrhea, and vomiting of the tension-surfeited infant—a relatively total response of the organism. Julius B. Richmond's work suggests that certain systems of the body are more reactive to stimuli than are others, and that this reactivity differs from individual to individual.[9] It may be, therefore, that those organs that are more reactive to increased tension that is not discharged have significance in the causation of later psychosomatic illnesses. Thus, as noted earlier, it appears that the neonate responds, relatively speaking, as a unitary rather than a differentiated organism. This undifferentiated response is particularly apparent when tension reduction does not occur, either because of the inefficiency of the individual's response competence or the failure of the external environment to supplement the neonate's limited resources.

Early Neurological Development

As a result of neurological development, memory traces which originally could be considered a type of conditioned reflex gradually become a function of the increasingly complex nervous system. This is a transition period that foreshadows the differentiation in function between the soma and the psyche. The first demonstrable change from undifferentiated to differentiated functioning is perhaps the

9. Julius B. Richmond, "Some Aspects of the Neurophysiology of the Newborn and their Implications for Child Development," in *Dynamic Psychopathology in Childhood*, eds. L. Jessner and E. Pavenstedt (New York: Grune and Stratton, 1959), pp. 78–105.

evidence of the neonate's "awareness" of tension and its nature. Evidence for this comes from the most reliable, though "unscientific," source—the nursery and the mother observer. Mothers are able, even in their infant's first few weeks of life, to differentiate the cry of hunger, of cold, of pain, or of "just crying." When they act on their often intuitive response to the infant's cry by providing that which they conceive to be the child's need, the crying stops. If one does not wish to accept this subjective observation of mothers, there is more objective evidence for this change. The hungry infant protesting against his discomfort will stop crying when he sees his bottle or is spoken to soothingly, or even when a person comes into his area of vision. It appears that there is a vague awareness of the nature of this discomfort, a memory trace indicating that the discomfort can be relieved through this visually or auditorially associated phenomenon and, on the basis of that memory trace, a brief decrease in tension or an increased tolerance for the tension occurs. Ultimately, too, delayed gratification results in the same massive discharge noted in the earlier period.

If gratification is gained, the accompanying relaxation does not necessarily lead to the earlier dormant state of the sleeping neonate. Now the infant may stay awake, move his arms and legs, make nonprotesting sounds. This state can be compared by analogy to the more mature state of "enjoyment." The infant is "aware" of the state of relief from discomfort. This awareness is not of a cognitive nature but, as the conception of biological memory traces would imply, a precognitive state. Freud has referred to this as the early stage of the unconscious, preceding as it does symbolic representation and thus conscious thought. This state of "awareness" precedes "perception," the latter term implying a "knowledge" of that of which the individual is aware. Perception also involves an affective response and thus is related to a more complex cortical functioning than one can hypothesize in the neonate.

Particularly in psychoanalytic literature, but also in other discussions of the psychological development of the individual, there are frequent references to the early period of life in which self and object are not differentiated. It is during this transitory stage of development in the first few weeks of life that there is an undifferentiated response to the object and the self. The infant experiences sensations that have internal origin as well as sensations that originate outside of himself, but he does not have the cortical development to differentiate their source. The anlage of that differentiation is present, however, in the specificity of the object stimuli to which he responds at about the fourth week of life. He responds to those objects which a memory trace associates with a release of discomfort, or to increased comfort. This development is accompanied by increased fussing.

Differentiation in the Function of the Psyche and the Soma

Further neurological development, particularly of the cortical centers, leads to the complete differentiation of function of the psyche and of the soma. In order to understand later disturbances, it is important to recognize, however, that this separation is never other than functional; the basic unity remains intact. The significance of this basic unity is only beginning to be explored. The most careful exploration so far has been that of Therese Benedek, in which the interrelationship of the reproductive glands and the psychological state was studied with results that demonstrated the fundamental interrelatedness of the soma and of the psyche.[10] The functioning of the adrenals, thyroid, and other glands of internal secretion affect the behavior of the individual in a way suggesting a change in psychic as well as somatic functioning. And psychic disturbances may result in somatic symptoms, as revealed in the study of psychosomatic diseases. There is growing evidence that sterility in males as well as in females and amenorrhea on a functional basis are sometimes related to psychological disturbances. Functional adrenal inadequacy may also be found to have a psychological component. It is on the concept of the unity of the specific parts of the total individual that Franz Alexander bases his theory that the true psychosomatic disorders are not conversion symptoms but actual symptoms resulting from a functional disturbance in one differentiated part of the organism affecting the functioning of another part.[11]

During the early stage of functional differentiation between the psyche and the soma, emotional responses gradually become discernible. They are not identical with the more mature affective responses but are forerunners of psychologically experienced "feelings." Attempting to place this phenomenon at an average age in development is difficult, at least at the present time. Mothers often claim to recognize a pattern of infant behavior that suggests an appropriate

10. Therese Benedek, *Studies in Psychosomatic Medicine: Psychosexual Functions in Women* (New York: Ronald Press, 1952).
11. Franz Alexander, *Psychosomatic Medicine* (New York: W. W. Norton, 1950), pp. 39–44, 65.

emotional response long before it is noted by the clinical observer. There are two possible explanations: First, the mother in her empathetic relationship with the child attributes to the infant feelings that she would have if exposed to the discomfort or frustration the baby is experiencing. Therefore, she interprets the baby's responses as evidence of his having those feelings. Second, the first evidence of affective response probably is an isolated occurence, one not necessarily repeated with the next similar stimulus situation; the clinician may not happen to be observing at the time when this fleeting emotional response occurs. Subject to wide variation in individual infants, and to wide variation in interpretation by adults, it would appear probable that an affective response rather than a primary functional response to pleasant and unpleasant situations begins about the third month of life.

The change in the nature of the infant's smile is an example of such a response as well as interesting to observe. The first "smile" of the infant is confined to mouth movements. It starts on the level of activity of the smiling muscles. The neurological development enables the infant apparently fairly early to have voluntary control of these muscles and thus to imitate the mother. It is interesting that this "smiling" appears to be one of the first imitative tools to develop in the individual and is related to the sense of "awareness" of external experiences. The original strained, affectless smile undergoes a rather rapid change, however, and soon to any observer's eyes the smile that earlier was a mere grimace now conveys the pleasurable feelings associated with the more mature smile. As the infant plays in his crib, exploring his hands or responding to the chance noise of a rattle, the smile will appear. It has now lost its imitative nature and has become a way in which pleasure is expressed.

Freud's conceptualization of the early infantile period included a description of infancy as a period controlled by the pleasure principle. He considered the recognition of reality as one of the early maturational steps of development. Once this recognition of reality occurs, the pleasure principle comes somewhat under the control of the reality principle and conflicts occur. This conceptualization appears to be an example of projection. An adult struggling with the vicissitudes of complex living imagines the infant's life as one dominated by pleasure and pleasure seeking, uncontaminated by conflicts over reality. As indicated earlier, however, early infant behavior appears to be determined by an instinctual urge to relieve discomfort by turning to external reality for gratification. Because of his limited neurological development, the infant does not "know" reality. To the same extent, however, he does not "know" pleasure. When the infant attains the neurological development that enables him to respond to the mother's face by temporarily ceasing his crying, he has in a limited sense become "aware" of reality. This enables him to anticipate relief of his displeasure because of his awareness of reality. To repeat and complete the previous quotation from Spitz, the first stage "is a stage which appears to be more biologically than psychologically understandable. *In the second stage pleasure is sought, unpleasure avoided and the pleasure-unpleasure principle has nearly unlimited sway over the infant.*"[12] (Italics added.) Is this not at least an *awareness* of the reality principle?

Actually, the infant always responds within the framework of reality even before he is aware of it. His awareness of reality and later his perception of it parallel his awareness of pleasure and displeasure. His later perception of reality is causally related to specific situations. From birth, however, he experiences his urge for a biologically comfortable state—the pleasure principle and the relief of his needs. His tools with which to solve the conflict are limited, but biologically he does the best he can with whatever he has. He uses his tools within the framework of reality.

Affective Responses

Affective responses become significant at about three months of age. Now the infant is aware of the stimulus that creates tension. He is aware of the tension and responds with displeasure, anxiety, and an anxiety response. If the tension exceeds his tolerance, he may respond by behavior typical of his earlier behavior or he may find relief of tension or a greater tolerance for tension because of secondary stimuli that are tension-reducing rather than tension-increasing. Because hunger has been previously used as an illustration, it will be used again, although many other stimuli now are becoming important. If the infant is hungry, he is aware of this discomfort and makes abortive attempts to relieve the tension created by the hunger stimulus. He puts anything available into his mouth and sucks on the object rather than crying, as he did earlier. If food becomes available, he will respond in the primary way by sucking the breast or bottle. Other stimuli, such as noise, the

12. Spitz, "Relevancy of Direct Infant Observation," p. 68.

appearance of another person, or sudden movements, either will not interfere with his sucking or will do so only briefly. The primary pattern of sucking is still dominant in contrast to the behavior of the somewhat older child who can usually readily be distracted from the eating activity.

The tension created by the hunger stimulus, however, can be either reduced or tolerated if a nontension-producing or a relaxation-producing stimulus is experienced, such as the mother's smile, the sight of the bottle, or being held. The infant becomes tolerant of a delay in gratification of the tension initiating the situation, undoubtedly in part because of a memory trace established by earlier gratification of a need. Accompanying this longer period of acceptance of delay in gratification, there is a more important maturational step. The infant is not only aware of tension; as it increases, he also responds to it with anxiety and displeasure-like behavior. Gradually, through the next months of his maturational development, these affective responses become more definable. From his behavior it becomes much more clear that he is anxious or displeased, the latter expressing itself as anger.

Lack of gratification also leads to an intensification of the original displeasure and anxiety. If chronic in nature, it results in a sense of insecurity; memory traces now become a part of the perceptive system and reinforce the tension that a stimulus creates because adequate relief is not a part of the past experience. In contrast, repeated tension-reducing gratification that leads to relaxation is responded to with pleasure. From this pleasurable state of relaxation evolves a sense of security, because past gratifications have been available to reduce tension. Hope of present and future relief has become a part of the infant's psychological makeup. Security, rooted in this hope, lessens the tension created by the stimulus and the infant's hunger tension remains within a limit that is not anxiety-producing.

As indicated above, hunger is not the only stimulus that creates this chain of events. Other behavior becomes understandable as having a goal and resulting in gratification. The infant begins, for example, to manifest more clearly the inherent drives that will be discussed in Chapter 6. When awake, if his relationship with other human beings has earlier been pleasant, he now "cries for attention." Thus, the alloplastic drive is no longer expressed only in terms of food but begins to take on the significance of primordial social contact. Progressively, his muscular and perceptive competence increases and the infant seeks aggressively that which will relieve or avoid discomfort. In spite of the clumsiness of his physical movements, his goal is clear. As he responds to the presence of a "loving, giving" person, he will arch his back even before he extends his arms in anticipation of the physical experience of being picked up and loved. This movement is soon replaced by reaching for the mother. These examples of behavior that are easily recognized by, although they undoubtedly precede, the sixth month of life, are not random, purposeless behaviors. They have a goal, and that goal is achieved by integrating the physical skills and the psychological needs. This manifestation of the drives is not a new development, but their expression is.

As indicated earlier, this metamorphosis does not occur overnight. It is a gradually evolving change dependent on the neurological (particularly cortical) development in combination with the actual experiences of the child. It is a maturational aspect of the human organism, and it also becomes more defined, demonstrable, and differentiated in specificity of response for some time after. Until the maturational change has begun to occur, however, the human organism is a biological or psychosomatic unit responding in accordance with the patterns of the primary functional level of development. It is when this beginning evolvement of the later level of maturation is reached at the psychologically functional components of the individual can be described separately from those that are functionally somatic. The child enters the oral phase of psychological development.

[4]

Oral Level
of Development

THE TERM "ORAL LEVEL OF DEVELOPMENT" is generally used in the scientific literature to refer to approximately the first eighteen months of life. But, as indicated in the previous chapter, the author considers the term "primary functional level of development" more accurate for the first few weeks of life. According to this conceptualization, the oral level evolves with the beginning of perception, the functional differentiation of the psyche and soma, and the experience of affective responses. These developments typically occur at about three months of age.

The above formulation is a tentative one. The infant's capacity to have an affective experience is hypothesized, but there is very little clinical material with which to test this hypothesis. There are certain clues in observable changes in the infant's behavior. If, for example, an older sibling has been consistently rough with the newborn, in a few weeks, and with the development of awareness, the infant will try to move away when the sibling approaches and he will start to cry. With the development of the early perceptive capacity, however, the infant may look frightened. This is certainly a subjective evaluation, but at least it is based on an observation that the facial expression has become different from the one that was observed a few weeks earlier under similar circumstances.

Another example suggesting that affective feelings accompany perception is the change that occurs in smiling. As also indicated in the previous chapter, smiling is perhaps first a motor response for which the stimulus cannot be detected and later a response in imitation of the mother's behavior. In the growth period now under discussion, the infant smiles in response to the perception of certain objects regardless of whether those around him are smiling; the smile is no longer imitative. It would seem justified to assume that the smile is a response to an internal feeling that is aroused by an external stimulus. In the infant's recent past, the smile was associat-

45

ed with a need-gratifying experience. With the capacity to be aware of pleasure, either associated with gratification of a need or independent of such gratification, the smile becomes a response to pleasure.

Sucking and Biting

It appears that, along with cognitive awareness of objects, the infant has now developed a capacity to be aware of and respond to sensations that are not simply those of physical comfort or discomfort. Certain feelings are experienced psychologically as distinguished from those experienced somatically. As indicated in the later discussion of erogenous zones (see Chapter 10), the oral level of development is characterized by oral erotism. The part of the body that produces the most gratification at this age is the mouth, particularly its sucking movements. Orality is often discussed as representing two stages of development: first, oral-receptive which corresponds with the time when stimulating the mouth mucosa initiates sucking, and second, the oral-aggressive or oral-sadistic, corresponding with the development of biting movements. The inclusion of the biting behavior in the functioning of the mouth is in part a reflection of neuromuscular development, especially in regard to the functioning of the tongue. During the early nursing period, the tongue's movement is such that it facilitates sucking but does not respond as it will later with movements characteristic of its use when solid food is being chewed and swallowed. As this latter function develops, there is possibly evolving a growing efficiency in the use of the mouth muscles involved in the forceful biting down that chewing represents. The function of the mouth becomes more than the holding role it plays in the early nursing period. This developmental step is discernible when teething is delayed. The infant will chew food, even though inefficiently, without teeth. Mothers are well aware of this phenomenon. A "teething biscuit" given to quiet the child while the bottle is being warmed is, if given early in the developmental period, sucked. Then comes the alarming day when a piece breaks off the biscuit and instead of sucking being responsible, the biting down of the gums upon the now semisolid substance is responsible. The infant does not choke on this relatively solid piece but chews until the biscuit softens sufficiently to be swallowed. This suggests that biting originally is not a psychological response but rather a physiological one made possible by neurological development. The biting response is usually stimulated by another development—the teeth are about to erupt. The discomfort of the swollen gums is apparently relieved by pressure through biting. Any object that is available is bitten.

It is because of the biting response of the infant at this age that this period has been referred to as one of oral aggression or oral sadism. Some attribute this behavior to the infant's awareness of the destructive significance of this gesture and that, therefore, he instigates it for destructive purposes. Others consider that the infant, having bitten down, recognizes his own destructive potentialities. If the infant is breast-fed during this time, the mother undoubtedly reacts with a startle response and may withdraw the breast. From this behavior on the part of the mother, the infant may gradually become aware of the potential for using biting against the mother. It is hypothesized from this recognition that the biting becomes a channel for the expression of an inherent aggressive impulse which is viewed as destructive. The impulse is eroticized, becoming thereby sadistic—sadism by definition being erotic gratification attained through acts of cruelty.

There are conflicting concepts regarding the origin of sadism in the literature.[1] The question involves whether masochism (erotic gratification from self-inflicted pain) is the basic pattern, with sadism evolving, by projection, from masochism, or whether the reverse sequence is true. The infant certainly experiences pain before he is able to inflict pain on another because pain is one of the fundamental tension-producing sensations. Pain is relieved in various ways during early infantile life, and relaxation results. On the basis of this sequence, masochism would appear to be the earlier response. But the tension of an eroticized experience is not normally characterized by unpleasantness but rather by pleasure because of the anticipation of relief. Pain from the tension becomes a factor only if the anticipation proves false. The pain of the infant's gums is not a self-inflicted pain; it is real. In the opinion of the author, the origin of the pleasure in masochistic and sadistic responses is a later ramification of the structural development of the psyche.

That the memory trace laid down by this early experience of pain and relief of pain through biting is later utilized symbolically—so that biting is both a masochistic and sadistic representation—is well

1. See for example, Charles Berg, *Clinical Psychology: A Case Book of the Neuroses and Their Treatment* (Mystic, Conn.: Lawrence Verry, 1948); Frederic Wertham, *Show of Violence* (Westport, Conn.: Greenwood Press, 1949); and Gerald C. Davison and John M. Neale, *Abnormal Psychology: An Experimental-Clinical Approach* (New York: John Wiley and Sons, 1974).

documented in the literature. The biting period during the oral stage of development, however, does not have the same meaning in actuality as it does later in the symbolism it provides. The early experience only provides a possible pattern for later psychological experiences.

Other Sensory Experiences

Early in his writings, Freud introduced a concept in regard to this early period, a concept that has received too little consideration. To describe the very young infant, he used the term being "polymorphous pervert." Perhaps the concept, so termed, carried implications that even his early followers could not tolerate. Consequently, the term, along with what it was intended to convey, was repressed until recently. Now it has again become a part of the conceptualization of the newborn. The phenomena to which the term applies are the multiple eroticized areas that can be identified in the young infant. Mild cutaneous stimulation, changes in equilibrium as the result of rocking movements, the sound of a soothing voice, and possibly all sensory experiences that are not too intense are indicative of the various erotic zones capable of producing overall relaxation when stimulated.

Although the satisfaction acquired from feeding involves the oral gratification gained from sucking, there would seem to be some justification for stressing other sensations experienced at the same time. An infant that is fed by propping up a bottle so that he can suck the nipple is being deprived of many aspects of a complete nursing experience, including physical contact with the mother. Textbooks on child development say that the neonate only sleeps and eats, but many babies fail to live up to the textbook standards! As the infant develops, even the textbook-compliant baby is awake increasingly between feeding periods. During the waking time, occasional periods of contact with another human being who is relaxed and warmly responsive to the infant foster the conversion of an "alloplastic" (that is, outgoing, interested in others) impulse to a drive to relate to other human beings. Furthermore, the basic need for care by a loving person becomes a need to be loved, and the gratification of this need provides the foundation for a sense of security. Therese Benedek has indicated that "the first regulator of self-esteem (the feeling of self as a whole being) is a sense of security acquired by the satisfactions connected with feeding."[2] To this probably should be added the sense of security that comes from other aspects of physical contact with a loving person. Were this not true, an infant physically cared for as far as nutrition and warmth are concerned would experience security through this limited meeting of his baby needs. But we do know that lack of adequate physical contact may create disturbances at the primary functional level.

Psychological disturbances and the origin of psychological scars may appear during the oral level of development. The infant may be unresponsive to his environment, suggesting possible retardation in development. He may also be chronically fussy and tense for no apparent reason. Certain children whose early infancy was characterized by psychologically sterile nutrition will later be fearful of external reality, showing no capacity to gain security through relatedness to others and learning, only after considerable time has elapsed, that they can be secure. In others, the alloplastic drive appears to have atrophied. They have no urge to find gratification in contact with others. Their need for love is satisfied through their love for themselves. In other instances there is an avoidance of relatedness to the external world—the most extreme example of which is the clinically psychotic child who is completely unresponsive to the world outside.

It has been argued that so long as the newborn infant's experiences are adequate, the identity of the caretaking person is not important; after all he is not able to identify this person. This is a fallacious use of the present knowledge of child development. The infant-care person plays an important role in the gradual functional differentiation of the infant's psyche and soma. As one phase evolves into another, the sameness of the environment, of the people about him who are caring for him, provides a continuum that parallels the continuum in his own development. In addition, one cannot say precisely that "today this particular infant will identify the person who cares for him."

If this continuum in the caring person cannot be provided, any deleterious effects can usually be corrected, and the consequences are not inevitably serious. This does not warrant, however, the attitude that there is no reason to prefer that a neonate be cared for by the person whom he will later come to identify as a valued object. With modern medical techniques many diseases can be cured; this fact,

2. Therese Benedek, *Insight and Personality Adjustment* (New York: Ronald Press, 1946), p. 10.

however, does not justify the attitude that it does not matter whether the individual gets a disease! Prevention is still the first choice of modern medicine.

Development of Perception

Paralleling, and closely related to, the oral phase of development, the instinctual response for survival undergoes a change. This change is brought about by the development of perception, which implies cortical awareness. As in all areas of development, this transition from one phase of maturation to the next is not sharply delineated. With cortical development the infant gradually comes to know—first in a very limited way and with later growth in an increasingly broader way—what a visual or other sensory experience means. When he responds to the sight of his bottle with urgency (whether pleasurably expressed or with increased tension) and assuming that his primary tension is created by hunger, it would seem justified to conclude that his capacity for perception is evolving.

During the earliest phase of the development of perception, recognition of the self emerges, a response which is usually referred to as a "sense of self." A sense of self is a psychological manifestation of the earlier survival instinct. In psychoanalytic terminology the affective response to the perception of the self is called "primary narcissism"; the origin of this term is found in the myth of Narcissus and his intense self-love.[3] Freud first described the state of early infancy as one in which all psychological energy is concentrated on the self. It is this pattern of use of psychological energy that he termed "primary narcissism."[4] Herman Nunberg states that the "self-preservative instinct is a narcissistic instinct whose function is to maintain the integrity of the personality and to protect it from injury."[5] Both of these definitions are in accordance with Hartmann's definition of primary narcissism as the sense of self. It is interesting

3. It is an unfortunate choice of words because self-love results in a striving to continue to live long after the basic survival instinct has lost most of its reflex patterns of discharge. It had disastrous consequences for Narcissus, but its absence would have equally disastrous consequences for the human being.
4. Sigmund Freud, "On Narcissism: An Introduction," *The Standard Edition of the Complete Psychological Works of Sigmund Freud,* vol. 14 (London: Hogarth Press, 1914), pp. 73–76.
5. Herman Nunberg, *Principles of Psychoanalysis* (New York: International Universities Press, 1955), p. 63.

that all these definitions imply a psychological structure in the newborn, attributing to the newborn organism a development of psychic responsiveness that one would question exists.[6]

What is the origin of primary narcissism? As noted in the previous material, the infant is a biological unit during the early neonatal period. The psyche and the soma are not separate entities; they respond in an undifferentiated way. The infant's energy is utilized chiefly in the maintenance of the biological state of living and biological growth: the intake of food to maintain energy, the discharge of unusable products of metabolism, a relative state of quiescence represented by sleep, and responses such as respiration, heartbeat, and the energy expended in other somatic manifestations that serve to maintain the continued life of the organism. Physical discomfort arises under conditions that are a threat to the biological organism. The discomfort results in reflex responses that are dependent upon the resources in, and the help from, the environment for their effectiveness in removing the threat and allaying the discomfort. Relief from discomfort creates a state of lessened stimulation and accompanying quiescence of the reflex responses. The survival threat no longer exists. The pattern of tension and reduction of tension is a biological state. If this is termed "narcissism" by the previously mentioned writers it should more accurately be modified to the term "biological narcissism," a synonym for the "instinct for survival."

Concept of Self

With cortical maturation and the growing capacity to identify cognitively the sources of sensory stimulation, the concept of the self evolves. Possibly the first step in this process is the cognitive differentiation of the self from the nonself. The neonate has internal experiences and experiences with external objects that foster or relieve his discomfort. René A. Spitz has indicated that, according to his observations, objects are not identified as such until the age of

6. The writings of the individuals quoted, when considered in more detail, indicate that this apparent adult-morphism is semantic rather than real. However, the inexperienced reader can be misled by the use of such phrases as "a narcissistic instinct whose function is to maintain the integrity of the personality."

eight months, but the infant is experiencing objects and is reacting to them long before that age.[7] This early period has been referred to previously as a period of "awareness." Thus, the preidentification period is characterized by experiences with objects that give comfort and serve for survival and those that create discomfort and threaten survival.

The philosophical implication of this concept is that effective boundaries must be established before the sense of self becomes possible. The infant's self-perception is significantly sharpened by the development of his concept of his body-self. As has been pointed out by Willie Hoffer, when the infant touches his body he experiences two sensations, that of touching and that of being touched. When he touches another object, he experiences only one sensation, that of touching. When he is touched by another object he experiences only being touched. As he enjoys exploring his own body and other objects and manipulating each, he has an additional experience. His body remains always with him, other objects come and go.[8]

During this early infancy period the self is defined gradually by another phenomenon: Discomfort from outside can be avoided. A precognitive example is the newborn's attempt to avoid the over-stimulation of bright light. In the first week of life the newborn will close its eyes in a poorly organized way in an attempt to counteract the stimulation. Some avoidance of an external stimulus that is either inherently unpleasant or unpleasant because of over-intensity is possible even in the early weeks of life. Internal discomfort cannot usually be avoided. There is no effective way for the infant to remove the discomfort of hunger.[9] Thus, need tension can be replaced by the tension-free state of satiation only by the nonself. Memory traces have been laid down earlier that now, with perception, enable the child to differentiate the self from the nonself.

The early separation of the self and the nonself is, however, far from complete. External objects become significant as they gratify the needs of, or threaten danger to, the child. As these external

---

7. René A. Spitz, *The First Year of Life* (New York: International Universities Press, 1965), p. 177.
8. Willie Hoffer, "Development of the Body Ego," in *The Psychoanalytic Study of the Child*, vol. 5 (New York: International Universities Press, 1950), p. 19.
9. There is a biological hunger avoidance phenomenon if hunger becomes extreme. Sensory pathways are blocked or sensory fatigue develops as a result of excess stimulation and the sensation of hunger disappears. This does not lessen the psychological hunger; it results only in the absence of sensation.

objects are identified, some are sought and valued. Their value lies in the roles they play; they are functional extensions of the self that assure the satisfaction of narcissistic needs. Those that jeopardize survival are rejected because of the threat they represent.

Other writers have offered quite different descriptions of this early phase of psychological development, the clearest contrasting conceputalization being Melanie Klein's formulation.[10] Klein views the early phase as one of oral incorporation in which the valued object (and in some instances a dangerous one) is made a part of the self by a fantasy of taking the object into the self. For example, she postulates a wish to take in and incorporate the breast into the self. [11] This formulation would seem to imply a more complex psychological structure at this time than is necessary; there would appear to be a simpler explanation. During this early period a narcissistically charged drive, the urge to survive, can be gratified only by an external object. The external object is valued not as an object per se but because of the function it serves. The breast is important because it is the source of nutrition. Thus, as it is recognized as an object, it becomes valued as one offering narcissistic gratification. Memories originating at this time undoubtedly lead to the psychological phenomena demonstrable in later psychological development, which are identified as incorporative and interjective tendencies, wishes, or behavior. Psychoanalysis does bring forth many dreams and fantasies concerning the breast. But it is a question as to whether these are memories uncontaminated by later knowledge that results in the breast becoming a symbol of the source of these early needs. Adults who were bottle-fed as babies also dream of breasts as a source of manna!

Significance of External Objects

The child becomes a psychological unit with an external object because of the extension of his narcissistic investment in the object which serves as a tool for the gratification of needs. Such objects are frequently referred to as "narcissistic love objects." This term implies that the object has no meaning to the individual except the functional one of gratifying a narcissistic need. This concept of the meaning of an object to a small infant would appear to shed light on

10. Melanie Klein, *The Psychoanalysis of Children* (New York: Grove Press, 1960), p. 11.
11. *Ibid.*

an observation in regard to child development: The first reaction to separation the infant manifests is a fear of losing a gratifying object, in contrast to a later fear of losing love and the object loved. During this early period, the infant responds as if he were losing a part of his extended self when the object disappears, that part of himself which is most significant for survival and the gratification of his many needs. He also responds as if the loss were permanent. Only after repeated experiences and with further development does he anticipate its return. Thus, the infant threatened with separation, if motorially sufficiently developed, will cling to the significant adult tenaciously, as if physical separation were to result in a total loss, and possibly total annihilation. This clinging behavior is demonstrated in the first year of life. It is probably the significant factor in the separation anxiety Spitz describes as occurring typically at eight months of age.[12] It may recur later when the child feels threatened by a life situation he cannot master and that he interprets as a threat to himself.

As has been mentioned previously, because of the significance of oral gratification in early infancy there is a tendency to overlook other gratifications that play an important role in this period. The small infant experiences reduction of tension and finally, with greater maturation, the psychological experience of pleasure as the result of movement, especially of a rhythmical nature, of cutaneous stimulation, and of sounds that originate from objects. Odor may also play a significant part in the early pleasure from objects. The narcissistic periphery of the child is thus extended through many of the child's experiences in addition to nursing. Many sources of gratification become a part of his narcissistically invested world.

A fixation at the oral stage of development is probably the core of a type of so-called psychopathic personality for whom the author uses the awkward phrase "being one's own best mother." These individuals do not present the characterological and personality picture of those usually clinically diagnosed as immature personality types. They are not clinging, self-depreciating, or immaturely self-aggrandizing. Superficially, at least, they function very adequately. They manipulate with great skill the people with whom they are in contact. If caught in a frustrating situation, they do not expose infantile fears and longings but rather an affective sterility in their response. They may express anger and disappointment but those

12. Spitz, *The First Year of Life,* p. 155.

responses lack the depth of affect that one would anticipate. There is an air of "It doesn't really matter." Other sources of gratification are quickly substituted for those that fail. The most striking aspect of their personality is that while people relate closely to them, they actually do not relate closely to people, except as people serve their needs. A person who no longer serves their needs is abandoned as if he or she were a toy. It would seem that these people are fixated (the author has never seen an example where it appeared to be regression) at a developmental stage at which the object, although separate from the self in form, is a narcissistic extension of the self and is valued only if it serves as such an extension; when it fails, it has no further meaning.

ᴄInherent Growth ᴄPotentials

THE CAPACITY FOR GROWTH is inherent in all young living matter, be it plant or animal. The typical pattern of the life cycle is one of balance between early rapid growth and gradual decay. Ultimately, the rate of decay is greater than the rate of replacement through growth.

This shift in balance is readily recognized in physical growth. Childhood encompasses three phases: infancy, latency, and adolescence. Infancy is characterized by very rapid physical growth. This growth process slows in latency, but in early adolescence there is another period of rapid growth. In adulthood little or no change ordinarily occurs in bone structure; the metabolic process ensures the maintenance of the body status quo. In advanced years, the metabolic process produces gradual changes and the body deteriorates.

There is a similar pattern in intellectual growth. Particularly during the first five years of life, the infant has the capacity for rapid intellectual development. He uses his ability to walk and he learns to talk. He learns the general meaning of his environment, how to explore it, and how to appraise what he explores. During adolescence, the rate of intellectual growth is often masked by emotional problems. Perhaps because of these problems, the adolescent's learning patterns change. His ability to think abstractly, to integrate many previously isolated feelings and experiences, and to plan for his future more or less realistically increases. This development is related to the effects of physical growth. The beginning functioning of the reproductive glands stimulates psychological as well as physical changes that ultimately lead to the attainment of physical and psychological adulthood.

In late adolescence, the intellectual potential realized becomes the final level of ability. Educational psychologists assume that intellectual growth ceases at approximately sixteen years of age. By that age the basic tools with which to learn are fully developed and there is no further evolvement of them during adulthood. With old age, the mental faculties often begin to decrease and senility may be a result.

A comparable growth pattern also occurs in emotional development. During approximately the first five years of life there is rapid emotional growth. Although emotional growth continues during latency, it is slower. During adolescence, there is a resurgence of psychological and emotional growth. With the completion of adolescence, adulthood is attained. At this time, emotional development reaches a level of relative status quo. Changes may occur under certain life situations, but these changes are only an enrichment of the basic adult psychological structure. With old age, the emotional level of development may undergo deteriorative change.

There is another aspect of this description of emotional growth yet to be explored. As indicated in Chapter 2, "The Parents," with the coming of parenthood there appears to be a further spurt of psychological growth in the relatively mature individual. It is yet to be determined that this is true growth; it may actually be utilization of previous growth which becomes focused with the onset of parenthood. This possibility is suggested in those instances in which childless people are able to manifest behavior similarly rooted but expressed in ways other than through actual parenthood. It may also be a growth potential which can be realized later than other elements of growth, remaining latent but to be utilized if an opportunity arises. That there is a point at which this growth possibility is no longer available is implied in the popular concept that parents who are older when their first child is born may have difficulty becoming parents psychologically, as parenthood is defined in the preceding material. A commonly held idea is that after a certain age one is too "set" in one's ways to become a parent easily.

Inherent growth potential can be crippled so that growth is arrested or distortions occur. Although there is a biologically inherent impulse to grow, problems may result if the proper nutrients to enable growth to take place normally are absent. Distortions resulting from inadequate emotional nutrition during crucial periods of growth become evident in the study of neuroses.

Normal physical growth responds adaptively to circumstances; it does not follow a stereotyped pattern. The scholar primarily interested in intellectual pursuits may be muscularly weak, while the miner develops strong muscles through constant use of his body. In each instance, the length of a muscle bundle has increased during the preadult period to adapt to the length of the bones between the attached ends of the muscle. That fact enables it to become the strong muscle of the miner while remaining undeveloped in the scholar; the growth of a particular muscle is determinèd by the use that is made of it. Thus, growth occurs not in a stereotyped way but according to specific need and use. The growth potential has been manifested within the framework of adaptation.

The adaptation of the growth process is also discernible in the intellectual area, and it is important to bear this in mind when evaluating behavior in terms of its psychological significance. For example, an individual in the process of maturing may consistently respond with more aggressive behavior patterns than would be considered valid under the circumstances of the evaluator's life situation. The evaluator then has a tendency to assume that this behavior is neurotic aggressiveness. However, the aggressive behavior may have been essential in the life situation of the particular individual. If so, his aggressiveness is not a distortion in his psychological growth, a neurosis; rather, it is a healthy adaptation to realistic demands.

Overall Picture of Human Growth

Construction of an overall picture of human development and maturation will make possible the summarization of material concerning the arrestive, the distorted, and the adaptive types of physical and psychological growth in the human being.

It is well recognized that adequate nutrition is essential for physical life. Without minimal nutrition an organism will die. Noxious agents can also destroy an organism. Nonfatal nutritional deficiencies or noxious agents may arrest growth, thus curbing the biological growth impulse sufficiently so that it is relatively ineffectual. The curbing of this impulse is seen not only in the stunting of physical growth by malnutrition, but also in the child's limited physical growth during a chronic illness. Frequently, however, the growth impulse is not completely curbed, and distortions in growth patterns occur. The development of rickets is an example; the bowing of the legs of a child suffering from a vitamin D deficiency occurs because the bone structure is growing in spite of the deficiency. This biological struggle to continue to grow results in a distortion of growth—bowed legs.

The adequacy of physical nutrition is also an important factor in intellectual growth. Crippling of the neurological system and particularly of the brain may be a result of inadequate nutrients for neurophysical development. Intellectual growth is dependent on intellectual nutrition as well, although it is difficult to differentiate this need from the dependency on stimulation.

Emotional growth is also a crucial aspect of the overall growth of the human organism. When the child has had inadequate or deleterious emotional nutrition, the result may be death, retardation, or distortions of growth. The interrelatedness of physical and emotional development can be documented. In some instances, extreme psychological deprivation has resulted in illness or death.[1] On the other hand, cases have been reported in which the physical aspects of the ill child's care were not modified but new psychological experiences produced a dramatic change from near fatality from the disease to recovery.

There are children who fail to develop a capacity to relate to others or to the object world because of a lack of emotional satisfaction in their early interpersonal relationships. This symptom is a failure in growth because this capacity to relate is part of the psychological orderliness of movement toward maturation. There are also children who show mild to severe distortions in emotional growth because of the inadequateness, either quantitatively or qualitatively, of their emotional experiences. This concept will become more significant and less platitudinous as the stages of emotional growth in the child are discussed in later chapters. One point should be stressed again at this time: Many distortions in emotional growth occur because the inherent impulse to grow remains active even though the nutrients are insufficient. The individual develops the emotional equivalent of bowed legs.

Stimulation in Growth

Another essential factor in growth is the availability of appropriate stimuli at the time the organism is able to respond to them. For example, parents often recognize that a child who crawls is likely to be delayed in walking or at least in developing his walking skills. Walking becomes possible as the result of neurological development, and that development is perhaps slowed when the stimulus of the

1. René A. Spitz, "Hospitalism," in *The Psychoanalytic Study of the Child,* vol. 1 (New York: International Universities Press, 1945), pp. 54, 59.

desire to get somewhere is met effectively by crawling rather than by the utilization of the more complex muscular patterns required to maintain the upright walking position.

As indicated earlier, the question of intellectual development is difficult to evaluate in terms of "nutrition" as compared to "stimulation" because, in the strictly intellectual area, these are synonymous. If stimulation-nutrition for the child is not available for intellectual growth, that aspect of growth may be arrested; whether it results sometimes in distortion of growth is not so easily determined. Arrested development is probably more common, or at least is the more easily identified result. The child who has always lived in an environment that does not nurture and stimulate him intellectually often will show an intellectual deficit that, until a certain age, is correctible if the child is then placed in an intellectually nurturing and stimulating environment. There are retarded children, however, who show unusual ability in specific areas. This may be an atypical development that has congenital roots, but it is also possible that in some instances it represents a distortion in intellectual growth and thus is an acquired unevenness that is the result of the particular type of stimulation-nutrition provided, correlated with the basic potential of the individual.

Stimulation is equally essential for emotional maturation. Corrective measures designed for the individual's best advantage are still being developed. Also, there appears to be a critical point in each aspect of emotional development beyond which recovery may be incomplete. There is material available that seems to demonstrate that lack of stimulation at the point at which an individual is emotionally ready to respond results in the atrophy of an inherent potential for healthy growth. When children are deprived of the stimulation that would foster maturation because of parents' needs or parental inadequacy, they fail to mature to the maximum of their potential. Margaret S. Mahler's study of the perpetuation of the symbiotic relationship between mother and child is a tragic example.[2] Less dramatic, but equally significant, the child who is ready for the next step in emotional maturation but who lives in an environment that does not stimulate, reward, or permit this next step will manifest either arrested or distorted growth at that point in his development.

2. Margaret S. Mahler, *On Human Symbiosis and the Vicissitudes of Individuation: Infantile Psychosis,* vol. 1. (New York: International Universities Press, 1968), p. 225.

Characteristics of Growth

There is, within broad limits, an orderliness in normal growth. Physically this is demonstrable in neurological development which advances from the cephalic to the caudal level. The development of neuromuscular control of the muscles of the head area occurs earlier than that of the musculature of the arms and trunk, which, in turn, precedes organization of the lower extremities that permits the complicated movements of walking. Such cephalic to caudal growth in intellectual development is not demonstrable at present except as it relates to neuromuscular development. Emotional development, however, does follow this progression in one particular area—that of the development of erogenous zones which progresses from the head (the oral) to the genitals. This progression is probably related in part to neural development.

There is another characteristic of growth that is important to bear in mind. The development of individual skills proceeds from the general to the specific. Physically this progression is apparent in the development of the use of the skeletal musculature. The large muscles early become serviceable to the wishes of the individual. At first their activity is nonspecific and serves only as a gross discharge phenomenon. Later the muscles become more specific in function, there is progressive use of the small muscles, and fine movements come into the service of the individual. A similar pattern exists in intellectual development. The young child reacts to the totality before he can understand the components of that totality. When, for example, he asks what the sky is, he is not inquiring about its composition, its relation to the universe, or why it exists. He is asking a much broader question; that is why his question is so impossible to answer. Only later is he curious about the details that make up the whole.

This latter concept is perhaps contradictory to a psychological concept that has long been accepted, namely, that the infant, as he begins to be aware of objects, relates to "partial" objects. An example is the theory, seemingly confirmed in the study of adults, that the infant relates first to the mother's breast instead of to the mother. The breast-fed infant undoubtedly has the most significant relationship with his mother through her breast; however, he experiences other gratifications at the same time that he is feeding. The bottle-fed baby has no breast to which to relate; yet, his early response to an object is not to the bottle but to the mother, who has in the past provided the bottle. This response can be verified when the appearance of the mother (or any person without the bottle) results in the temporary cessation of crying. Only later will he respond specifically to the sight of the bottle.

The infant's emotional response also proceeds from the general to the specific. The needs of the neonate are total needs and their frustration brings forth a pattern of total response. The hungry infant responds by crying, by kicking, and by general body tension. As maturation results in the differentiation of psychological needs from physical needs, this total response to frustration continues for a time; however, when deprived of emotional gratification, the infant may develop an anaclitic depression as conceived by René A. Spitz—that is, a response of the total organism.[3] Only with gradual maturation do the needs become differentiated, the gratification for the needs more specifically sought after, and the response to frustration more specifically manifested. Thus the six-year-old child experiencing a need for dependency gratification will seek it from a parent or parent substitute; if he longs for social contact he will seek it from his own age group. A general need for a relation to others has become differentiated into component parts and the solution has also developed specificity. If this is borne in mind in evaluating the response of the neonate, for example, there will be some safeguards against interpreting the neonatal behavior in terms of an adult conceptualization.

In the preceding material a physical, intellectual, and emotional growth are discussed as separate entities, but such a separation is artificial. The child's development in any of the three areas will be affected, to a greater or lesser extent, by factors affecting the other two areas. For example, a child who suffers from a seriously debilitating physical illness often will show retardation in intellectual and emotional development. And a child whose intellectual potential is not being fulfilled because of lack of intellectual nutrition and stimulation may show a comparable delay in emotional maturation. At times it is difficult to assess whether the factors that led to intellectual arrest also led to emotional arrest, or whether the one affected the other. Wisely handled, a child who has limited intellectual potential will manifest emotional maturation. His intellectual limitations do not appear to have the same effect as is sometimes

3. René A. Spitz, *The First Year of Life* (New York: International Universities Press, 1965), p. 272.

observed in cases of arrested development or unfulfillment of the potential of the inherent intellectual endowment. The effect of the interrelatedness of physical, intellectual, and emotional growth can be appraised only by a study of the individual case. A generalization is not warranted.

Importance of Inherent Characteristics

The universality of the growth phenomenon is not the only aspect to be examined when attempting to facilitate optimal growth in an individual. There is a current popular belief that a child at birth is like a piece of putty and becomes a recognizable structure only as the result of the molding influence of others. Even the physical aspect of development has not been spared. Because adequate nutrition promotes optimal physical growth and inadequate nutrition results in less growth than is possible, parents can, in good faith, tell a child that "he must eat to grow tall." In fact, the child can, with adequate nutrition, only reach the fulfillment of his own growth potential; he will not exceed it. The putty theory has had consequences more serious than the feeding problems that may result from universal parental use of this observation concerning physical growth, that appear, within limits, to be justifiable. It has created a serious fallacy in regard to psychological growth.

That physical and emotional nutrition, both of which are controlled by others than the child, play an important part in healthy maturation can certainly be validated both by laboratory and clinical research. This fact, however, does not necessarily have as its corollary that *only* what others do explains the ultimate picture. Nobody questions that the seed of a plant contains in it a certain potential for becoming that plant. Its growth will be influenced by many conditions, but the seed is not like a piece of undifferentiated putty. If the seed is from a bittersweet vine, it will not become a honeysuckle vine because someone tends it as though it were a honeysuckle vine. It will respond to whatever care it receives as a bittersweet vine. It may become a flourishing, a weak, or a rambling, straggly vine. The ultimate picture will be determined by many factors, both inherent and environmental, but the seed was the embryonic form of the bittersweet vine and it can grow only into some configuration of a bittersweet vine.

This leads to a question: What is inherent in the germ plasm which will affect the ultimate maturation of the human individual? There are certain inherent potentials which may fail to develop, may only partially develop, or may reach the optimal level of development under the most favorable circumstances. However, the individual cannot exceed the level of his own inherently determined potentials.

From the psychological standpoint the most obvious aspect of the inherent capacity of the individual is to be seen in a consideration of his intellectual potential as a newborn infant. There are congenital differences in intellectual potential. As the child develops, his intellectual potential will become demonstrable. Mental retardation may be the result of an inherently limited intellectual potential, but other facts are also important in preventing the development of this potential. For example, emotional problems may retard intellectual growth. Or, a brain injury from physical trauma or from a noxious agent such as that involved in encephalitis may affect parts of the brain that have to do with intellectual functioning, and further development will either be slow or absent.

Intellectual development early in life may seem to be accelerated beyond the child's potential as the latter is manifested later. There are small children who, because of the stimulation they receive from their environment, respond in a manner suggesting very superior intelligence but who fail to maintain that superiority in spite of continued stimulation. A case in point is that of Johnny who, at the age of two and one-half years, had an intelligence quotient of 172. At six, without a discernible change in the environment, his intelligence quotient was 130 and remained there in subsequent tests. This discrepancy was due in part to the inadequacy of testing material for the very small child, but it is doubtful that such a wide discrepancy can be fully explained in that way. He walked at eight months and spoke in sentences with the correct use of pronouns and verb tenses at eighteen months. A more likely explanation for the discrepancy is that for that period he had been the constant companion, source of gratification, and conversational partner of his mother, who was temporarily separated from her husband by the war. She was an intellectual, verbal person and lived in almost complete isolation from other adults. The stimulation that this situation provided probably resulted in a pseudo-acceleration of development which could be maintained for only a short period of time.

There is another situation in which it appears that intellectual development fails to continue. Certain children, either because of their environment or for some other reason related to their own adjustment to life, invest a great deal of their available energy in learning. These children may have a brilliant career in the early part of their school life. Because many school systems up to the college level do not evaluate or demand the child's full use of his capacity for independent thinking, his school performance is evaluated on the basis of rote learning. The early school period provides the child with tools which will serve the purposes of later creativeness. A school that stimulates the creative thinking of its students and values the child's achievements when he responds to this stimulation does not serve its purpose if this is all that it does. A criterion for achievement in the early school period is the child's effective development of skills with the three "Rs" and the learning of facts to which this development leads. Those children who become skilled in the use of the basic tools and gain a grasp of the relatively unembellished facts that these tools make available to them may receive quite adequate grades, suggesting that they would profit by a college education. In college, however, they soon find themselves lost, especially if the college has a different criterion of achievement from that of the earlier school. The young person's failure may have disturbing results. At a time that is most difficult for him (late adolescence), he must revise his plan for his adult life and do so under the stress of seeing himself a failure.

From a practical standpoint these children should be identified early by testing under conditions most conducive to bringing out their full potential in order to avoid the later problem. From a theoretical standpoint these children do not represent an example of early rapid intellectual growth which becomes slower later in childhood. Rather, they are an example of the full use of intellectual potential which later, even though utilized to the full, cannot meet the demands of broader areas of learning.

The intelligence of the infant is often evaluated on the basis of the time at which he rolls over, sits up, walks, and talks. The timing of these accomplishments is only a very rough index of developmental potential. The infant who is large and heavy often walks at a later age than does a slender, petite child. The former infant's body build demands more of his legs than does the physical build of the latter. An infant learns to talk partly to communicate. If the infant can communicate effectively by other means, has no incentive to communicate verbally because of the nature of his environment, his speech will be delayed. Late speech does not necessarily indicate mental retardation. Several factors must be present and the overall life situation understood before a child's intellectual potential can be evaluated. Regardless of postnatal circumstances that affect the growth of a child's intellect, intellectual potential is an inherent characteristic which can be damaged but never permanently increased.

Another aspect of intellectual potential is the question of talent. It appears that an individual may be born with talents in certain areas which will become significant in accordance with the use he and his environment make of those talents. Many talents undoubtedly are a combination of fortuitous capacities. A future singer, for example, must be able to "carry a tune." Some people apparently are congenitally defective in that skill. The singer must have a voice box that can produce vibrations that are musical; training only perfects the use of the voice box. If these inherent capacities are developed, the individual can become a singer. Without the congenital concomitants and the interests and opportunities to develop the talent, the individual will not become a singer. It is more difficult to say where one draws the line in fields that do not involve such obvious ancillary equipment. At present there is no conclusive answer to the question whether a successful writer and an equally successful mathematician become successful in their respective fields as a result of later factors that determine the choice of activity, or whether the "genius" is a combination of inherent intelligence and life experience.

In addition to intellectual endowment, there appear to be other inherent characteristics that are less easily documented but that differ from individual to individual. These differences may influence the patterns that evolve with development and maturation. For example, there appears to be a congenital difference in the energy endowment (to be discussed in Chapter 7) that is evident from birth. Some newborns sleep as the book says they should; others have more waking time and yet are not fussy babies. This difference may be related to energy endowment, with the wakeful baby having more energy reserve and thus requiring less sleep. As these babies with contrasting behavior reach a few weeks of age, their differences appear to be due in part to their environment. The question then arises whether the environment responds differently to the difference in the children and thus increases the contrasting behavior. The baby that sleeps a great deal receives less attention from the parents. A wakeful baby stimulates parental interest and eventually finds such interest a very pleasant experience. He can become not necessarily the quiet, awake infant, but possibly a fussy infant who, during wakefulness, attracts adult attention by his fussiness.

There is another difference in the responses of the newborn that may have later significance. Some neonates are more muscularly active than others. Although it is difficult to be certain that observations of the newborn are accurate, some neonates when awake and fussy appear to express their protest in more violent muscular discharge than others whose crying is accompanied by minimal physical activity. There is perhaps a congenital difference in the way neonates discharge biological tension.

A final difference that is probably also congenital is the strength of the instinctive responses in general and the difference in the strength of one drive in contrast to others. This is only a tentative postulation, based chiefly on later observation. For example, one newborn will suck avidly at the first opportunity; another will be relatively indifferent and will suck only under the stimulus of hunger. This contrast in behavior is not necessarily related to basic energy endowment, because some infants in the first category sleep the conventional amount of time while those in the second category are peaceful, motorially active, wakeful infants.

It is not always clear why two people under broadly similar circumstances react differently. One person, faced with a crisis, will aggressively attack the problems presented; another will submit to the consequences, finding effective means to avoid damage to himself in so doing. If one is knowledgeable of the early life histories of those involved, an early experience or a series of experiences that appear to explain the difference can frequently be found. Often, however, the question is: Why did the two people, even in those early experiences, react so differently? For example, babies exposed to mothers who have a minimal capacity to love an infant will manifest the deprivation involved differently. One will be fussy and try to get some kind of response from his environment. At the other extreme, a baby may make no protest, becoming an alarmingly unresponsive infant. A third infant may be a truly "good" baby, apparently absorbing what little is available from the mother with effective results.

Mothers verbalize such difference in their own infants too often for one to assume that their observation is related only to their own limitations as a mother. Mothers who have been able to be relatively warm in their response to one infant will state, in one way or another (depending on their level of sophistication), that another infant somehow did not arouse in them the same feelings. "He wasn't cuddly." "He didn't seem to care if I was around or not." "All he wanted of me was food." "He seemed angry from birth on." "He fought everything I did for him." "He just wasn't an appealing baby like the other child was." These are typical comments of mothers in the latter instance.

If further study indicates that there is this difference in the nature of the neonatal response, it is undoubtedly the first coil of a vicious spiral, especially if the parents are immature or ill-equipped for parenthood. The neonate who does not arouse parental feelings in adults who are essential to him becomes a deprived infant. His mode of handling that deprivation may be an intensification of his primary response, which increases the emotional distance between him and his parents. Later, when his personality becomes more complex, the core of the difficulties that arise can be found in the failure of the parents to meet his emotional needs effectively. Undoubtedly, the emotional problems of the parents were in part responsible, but the congenitally determined and early manifested nature of the neonate's response may have been a significant component in the later unfortunate relationship between parent and child.

Further study of the neonate may suggest other inherent characteristics that become a part of the ultimate psychological format of the mature individual. That there are such inherent characteristics does not imply, however, that the neonate is doomed to have a predefined personality configuration. These inherent characteristics are only the stones of a foundation. As such, they provide a certain gross framework on which many varieties of personality can be built. An individual, because of his genes, may not grow taller than five feet six inches. At that height, however, he may be a slender, muscularly weak individual, or he may, through exercise, develop powerful muscles that will enable him to perform tasks that a tall person with undeveloped muscles cannot do. Many factors that come into play after birth will determine what an individual does with his inherently determined physical structure.

It may be equally true that other inherent patterns are affected by later experiences. Certain children may have an inherent pattern of reaction in which motorial discharge is prominent. Such a child may become a person who faces every crisis by physical fighting, or one who develops motor skills but lives peacefully, or one who inhibits motor activity because early experiences proved to result in painful consequences, or one who enjoys *doing* physically rather than just sitting and thinking. Certain children may be more sensitive and responsive to interpersonal relationships than others and may present a variety of personality configurations later. Such a child may develop into a person who manifests his sensitivity through a tendency to have his feelings hurt by any nonpositive social relationship. He may develop into an artist, given other components that enable him to do so, thus expressing his sensitivity esthetically. He may become an adult who, because of his own sensitivity, is sensitive to the needs of others and thereby utilizes his basic sensitivity in the understanding of these needs. On the other hand, his sensitivity may have proved so painful to him that he has placed a check on it and, like the motorially active child who experienced too serious consequences as a result of his early activity and repressed his motor activity, he may repress the earlier responsiveness and appear to be quite insensitive. Thus, the concept of inherent differences in individuals does not invalidate the concepts of those interested in the effect of postnatal experiences on the development of the child as he grows to adulthood. It only implies that the ultimate end of the growth process may be affected by the inherent psychological structure which served as the foundation.

[6]

Inherent Needs
and Drives

EVERY LIVING THING HAS certain basic needs which must be satisfied in order to maintain life, and there are responses stimulated by those needs that enable their fulfillment. This urge to live expresses itself through instinctual responses characteristic of the species; responses that meet the inherent needs of the particular living organism. For example, certain plants need light in order to survive; thus, they grow toward the light. These inherent responses to certain needs, if used repetitively and proven effective, become the basic components of adaptation.

The simpler forms of animal life have less complex survival needs and simple patterns of adaptation. The higher forms of animal life have more complex needs and the potential for a more complex adaptive pattern. Man has the most complex inherent needs and, because of his basic mental characteristics, a greater capacity to adapt to complex situations. The core of his adaptive pattern, however, is identical to that of all living organisms—the inherent urge to survive and the instinctual response to this urge that is essential for survival.

The human infant is born "prematurely" in the sense that, compared to all other animals, he is the least able—and for the longest period of time, unable—to fulfill those needs essential for survival, and he has relatively few innate behavior patterns. In species dependent for survival on nursing, René A. Spitz cites the rooting instinct of the newborn as an instinct expressed through a reflex response that is essential for survival.[1]

During the neonatal period, as maturation takes place, the effect of these inherent needs and responses on the development of the personality of the individual makes it possible to identify them more definitely. Our present knowledge of the significance of neonatal

1. René A. Spitz, *No and Yes: On the Genesis of Human Communication* (New York: International Universities Press, 1957), pp. 23–29.

responses and their later evolution as discernible in the more mature psychological structure does not provide sufficient material to be certain that all innate responses can be identified; it would appear, however, that there are at least four inherent responses that are essential for survival. These responses are related to four needs that are significant in the ultimate psychological development of the individual.

The Alloplastic Drive

All living things turn to outside sources for need satisfaction. This alloplastic drive is most clearly demonstrated biologically in the fact that an organism is dependent on its environment for nutrition; the mere presence of nutrient substances does not assure their utilization, and there must be a mechanism that allows the organism to take in these substances. For example, the rooting and the sucking responses in the nursing neonate result in an intake of milk. Baby chicks peck at objects and, while pecking, they learn which objects will satisfy their hunger. The specific form the response to a specific need takes is determined by the biological heritage of the organism and the reality situation. This is one aspect of an inherent alloplastic drive which is in the service of survival.

Not only does the mode of expression of the alloplastic drive vary from species to species, but so does the nature of the stimulus that triggers it. John Bowlby describes the very early mother-child relationship as one that is characterized by object sucking and object clinging.[2] Clinging seems to be a universal characteristic of primate infants. Although mothers in the higher primate species play a role in holding their infants, those in the lower species do little for them and the infants must cling to their mothers' bellies to remain with them. Thus, in the wild the infant's life literally hangs on the efficacy of its clinging response. Although the human infant does not cling in this fashion, a residual is seen in the grasp reflex of the human neonate.

Many infant animals will cease crying when they are held. A small puppy, when first separated from its mother and its litter, will cry day and night unless it is comforted by contact with another living being. Crying human infants respond to fondling, caressing, or gentle patting when, at least as far as it can be determined, their cry is not

2. John Bowlby, "The Nature of A Child's Tie to His Mother," *International Journal of Psychoanalysis* 39 (1958): 350–71.

related to the intensity of hunger discomfort. This suggests a particular characteristic of the alloplastic drive as seen in certain higher animals, especially in man. Turning outward for gratification is not only determined by an inherent biological need for nutrition and warmth, it is also determined by a need for contact with another living being who can respond adequately to the implied need.

As the human infant matures beyond the neonatal period, evidence of the alloplastic drive becomes more demonstrable even though it is conditioned by life events and colored by fusion with other inherent drives. In the first year of life a child develops sufficient motor coordination to enable him to satisfy any need he might have for cutaneous stimulation. He can pat himself almost as efficiently as his mother can; however, except under pathological conditions it is his mother's patting, not his own, that comforts him. With further development he can gratify a number of other longings: He can suck his thumb, masturbate, and eventually find his own food. At times he will do all of these things, but the absence of another person leaves him dissatisfied. For example, a psychologically healthy child may, under certain conditions, suck his thumb. He will abandon his thumb, however, if other satisfactions are available from his environment. Clinically, excessive thumb-sucking is evaluated as an indication of some chronically frustrated need of the child. It is often indicative of a sense of insecurity associated with inadequate experiences in an affectively meaningful exchange with a mother figure. The need to be loved is inherent in the human species, but this need is expressed in terms of being loved by *someone else.* Thus, the basic need to be loved finds gratification through an alloplastic response. The built-in satisfaction source, the thumb, is only a substitute for what is really sought.

The alloplastic drive finds mature expression in later social behavior. Human beings are, in a refined sense, "pack" animals; social interchange is important to them. This phenomenon has been explained as having a phylogenetic origin. As the prehistoric caveman became aware of other cavemen and also aware that he was inadequate to deal with animals more powerful than he, he supposedly discovered that two men against one animal had a better chance than either man had individually. Thus, social structure came into being. Man became, according to this theory, a pack animal that evolved into the social being of historic time; his socialization is a phylogenetic heritage. It can be questioned, however, whether a pattern of behavior is phylogenetically retained only because it had a pragmatic function in the past. Rather, may it not be retained because it meets some inherent need of the organism, a gratification of that need at having different pragmatic values different times?

Most people can tolerate separation from others briefly, but when it extends beyond a time span that exceeds a particular individual's tolerance threshold, loneliness is experienced. Loneliness is a very painful emotion and it would seem to stem from a longing for gratification of a basic need that is unmet. Often small children enjoy imaginary companions, especially when circumstances isolate them from contact with other children. There are many significant aspects to the role of an imaginary companion. Why is it that most often what is chosen is another child or an animal most nearly providing the type of gratification sought from human beings? The small child may carry on a casual conversation with an imaginary companion in the same manner he might talk to a living child. It is interesting to note that imaginary companions sometimes come into being before the age when the child ordinarily shows a capacity for real social relationships with his own age group. Later, the level of social exchange with the imaginary companion is frequently more advanced than the child's actual behavior with live companions! Social relationships may have an earlier basis than their apparent origin in primitive man's need for help.

If a social response is a phylogenetic heritage, why was it selected to be retained? It would seem logical to assume that socialization is a characteristic of human behavior in part because of an inherent urge to turn outward for the gratification of internal needs. The needs take a form having certain characteristics that are uniquely human. They are adaptable in their form of expression to the exigencies of the moment.

This concept of the alloplastic drive's having goals broader than the gratification of immediate specific needs would, if valid, offer a partial explanation of why the environment, particularly the people composing the environment, are so significant in the psychological development of the individual and why so much of the psychological configuration of an individual is expressed through his response to the environment. Modern child-rearing and educational methods stress the importance of the child's social development. The implication is that this development must be imposed through instruction—perhaps a fallacious approach to the fostering of socialization. If there is an inherent need for social relationships and an inherent drive to fulfill that need, the part that the child-rearing and educational approaches should play is that of encouraging and directing the expression of a pattern of behavior that already, in embryonic form, is a part of inherent human activity. When a child fails to show social adjustment commensurate with his age, it is perhaps not a question of *how* to teach him to socialize but rather *what* is inhibiting the response that is characteristic of the human species.

The Love-Seeking Drive

The human species appears to have, as a component of the instinctual response assuring survival, a type of reaction to certain stimuli that ultimately is equated with the concept of love. Love is considered a human characteristic, and other animals are given credit for that capacity only when they seem to react like human beings, however, many higher forms of animals probably experience affectively something comparable to human love. From the standpoint of the survival of most species some form of positive acceptance by another is essential, even though it may be expressed only by coitus.

For those animal species in which nursing is the source of nutrition for the young, physical contact with another is essential for the species' survival. In the human species breasts are the biological source of essential nutrition but nursing is a more complex experience than just deriving nutrient gratification. The extent and significance of other facets of the experience, although important to all nursing species, are especially important to the human species.

The human infant has to be held to be fed from the breast. Thus, the gratification of a survival urge—the need for food—is accompanied by many kinds of sensory stimulation. The sensation of being held, the warmth of the mother's arm, the sight of her face, the sound of her voice, and the rhythmical movement of her body all contribute to the infant's feelings of security.

Although cutaneous stimulation is essential to the newborn of many species, for less complex animals it is of shorter duration and is a less all-encompassing experience than it is for the human infant. It would appear that the body sensations that accompany infant care have an importance to the total organism beyond chance significance. A suggestion of the importance to the development of the newborn of the fulfillment of the need for sensory stimulation is implied in the historical development in the patterns of infant feeding. Scientific studies of the needs of the newborn have resulted in the development of formulas that adequately meet nutritional needs, and bottle feeding has become a common practice. However, parents are usually advised by pediatricians that bottle feeding should simulate breast feeding as nearly as possible, and it is recommended that the infant be held in a nursing position. If the human infant is critically deprived of those sensory experiences that typically accompany breast feeding, his development may be retarded, irrespective of the adequacy of the nutrition provided. This failure to develop properly is demonstrable in certain types of pseudo-mental retardation, in certain types of infantile psychoses, and in the practically extinct picture of marasmus. What is significant apparently is not the source of nutrition but the conditions under which the nutrition is provided. Because the person who most effectively provides this biological experience is the person who loves the infant, it is said that the infant "needs love." More correctly, he needs the biological experience that can only be provided adequately by a loving person.

It is difficult to determine whether the neonate biologically experiences not only nutritional hunger but also "hunger" for sensory stimulation. The atypical behavior of certain infants who do not have a positive experience through contact with others in spite of adequate nutritional intake suggests such a "hunger" may exist. If this is true, it would explain the reduction of tension when such sensory stimulation is provided. The reduction of tension, or, to put it more positively, a state of relaxation, is the biological equivalent of the psychological state of a type of primary pleasure. With further development this neonatal experience leads to the response of seeking love and, ultimately, of loving in a mature person. The sensation of primary pleasure from contact with another is the anlage of the affective response to being loved and of loving.

This contact during infancy with a loving person is accompanied by stimulation of the early erogenous zones. Thus, the pathway for the evolvement of erotic love is established, to find expression in maturity in sexual love as well as in sublimation of the sexual component in love for those who are not sexual objects. It has been assumed that, in the mature individual, all love for others is an indication of a sublimation of erotic love, if it is not overtly sexual. Further exploration may prove that mature, directly nonsexual love is actually an entity in itself. The response of love may be an expression of an inherent impulse that with maturation has led to the love-need being expressed under one set of circumstances through erotic love, under other circumstances through nonsexual (not desexualized) love. This would not invalidate the observation that many manifestations of apparently nonsexually charged love are actually a sublimation of sexual love; it would only indicate that not all nonsexual love is the result of sublimation. This conceptualization is valid only if libidinal energy is considered energy that is channelized to express a libidinal impulse but which can also be utilized for other forms of expression.

The alloplastic drive and the love-seeking drive are closely interrelated. In certain aspects of early infant behavior they become fused. Clearly, the need for those satisfactions provided by a loving person can be adequately met only by turning outward, but, as indicated earlier, were the alloplastic drive not present, the infant, by his own activity, eventually could satisfy those needs that are satisfied by a relatedness to others. And were the need for love from others not present, the infant's contact with his external environment as well as with his internal self would, to state it broadly, be devoid of "humanness."

The Aggressive Drive

A third inherent response which serves the purpose of survival is the aggressive drive. Stated more accurately, this is a drive for which the ultimate goal is mastery, but in its earliest form it is manifested as a response to discomfort. Only later does it become associated with mastery for which active discomfort is not necessarily the trigger but rather the seeking of pleasure and avoidance of displeasure.

The crying and intense random muscular activity when the newborn is physically uncomfortable are usually explained as a massive discharge of tension resulting from the frustration of certain needs. This explanation of the infant's behavior solely as a tension reducer is not entirely convincing. As one watches an infant who is crying and moving about, exhibiting disorganized motor activity, it appears that the longer the need—hunger, for example—persists, the greater the intensity of the activity becomes. Furthermore, if the need is met—food is provided, for example—the massive discharge ceases immediately. Hunger undoubtedly does not disappear with the first swallow of milk, but manifestations of frustration do.

This pattern of behavior suggests that there is an inherent aggressive drive to seek the satisfaction of biological needs, again a response that serves the need for survival. The newborn's reaction to discomfort is a primitive expression of this instinctive response. Because of the infant's lack of biological development, the impulse cannot be expressed in a sufficiently integrated way to achieve its end unless external factors provide a particular type of stimulus. If the nipple stimulates the sucking reflex, and if food flows, the infant in cooperation with the outside world has found a satisfactory outlet for the inherent need to seek relief aggressively; tension is dissipated.

The infant is frequently described as passively receptive. This is not so. He actively expresses his aggressive drive. He does not lie in a completely passive state while manna flows from heaven into his mouth without any active participation on his part. Considering his capabilities, the neonate is relatively more aggressive than any mature organism, and food intake is an excellent illustration. When the infant is hungry, that stimulus results in a demonstrable chain of events. Once the mother has picked him up, he begins to root, a response that results in finding the breast. He begins sucking, and that response drains milk from the breast if it is available. Only if his hunger cannot be gratified by these aggressive steps does he respond with crying and expressing his discomfort in random movements. Passivity that is recognized in the mature personality is not an outgrowth of infantile nursing but is rather an outgrowth of dependency on the external world once the active response is instigated. Babies who are less active in attaining satisfaction are not truly passive; they are simply infants in whom the aggressive element of the survival instinct is less strong. Willingness to receive should not be equated with passivity unless one differentiates the so-called passivity as represented by the receptiveness of the infant from the passivity of the adult personality.

The use of the term aggressive drive has resulted in its being conceptualized in diametrically opposite ways. The aggressive drive is defined by many as being a destructive drive in its primitive form. It was so defined by Freud in his concept of the death wish, but the concept underwent many modifications during his creative lifetime. He states, "We may suppose that the final aim of the destructive instinct is to reduce living things to an inorganic state. For this reason we call it the "death instinct."[3] Hostility, self-destruction, and destructive impulses toward others evolve from this basic instinct.

An alternative concept of the aggressive drive, the one that is implied in the preceding paragraph, assumes that in its primitive form the aggressive drive is expressed as an impulse to respond

3. Sigmund Freud, "An Outline of Psycho-Analysis," *The Standard Edition of the Complete Works of Sigmund Freud,* vol. 23 (London: Hogarth Press, 1964), p. 144.

actively to unpleasant situations and to seek direct gratification of a
need, later to become also an act of seeking pleasure and avoiding
pain. The apparent destructive component of the drive, then, is not
the drive itself. Rather, the destructive component is the result of the
inadequacy of the child's equipment to deal with the tension resulting
from the failure of discharge of the basic drive. This response to
frustration of the aggressive drive later becomes recognizable as
hostility. Aggression is not then de-aggressified when constructively
channelled; it is simply more effectively utilized and frustration is
avoided.

The latter concept would seem to be more applicable to understanding infant and child behavior than is the former concept,
according to which one would anticipate that a nonfrustrated infant
would show minimal aggressiveness. This is so if one looks on
aggressiveness as hostility; a relatively nonfrustrated infant is a
relatively relaxed one. But a nonfrustrated infant is also a more
responsive infant; he nurses better and, as he matures, he more
readily accepts short frustrations such as brief delays in feeding. The
frustrated infant is fussier at first but is inclined to give up if the
frustration is too chronic and too intense. In early infancy, marasmus
develops; in a slightly older child, an anaclitic depression. These two
conditions can result from the fact that the aggressive drive is finally
defeated by continuous frustration.

The final biological renouncement of drive can be brought about in
other ways as well. For example, the child is given physical sustenance but without the biologically essential component of what can be
referred to as "tender, loving care." The infant seeks food aggressively by sucking, but progressively becomes tense over the lack of
the "love" components and, unable to find a way with his primitive
tools to get that form of nourishment, he becomes fussy and restless.
Two instinctive needs are frustrated, the need for care by a loving
person and the need for relief from the tension that frustration
incites. The aggressive impulse has reached an intensity of stimulation that exceeds the infant's tolerance and no responses to the
stimulation occur. The aggressive impulse in these particular infants
succumbs before that of nursing. The latter is also finally defeated
and the infant dies of malnutrition.

In more mature behavior than that of the neonate it would seem
possible to understand how hostility is aroused when the aggressive
response of the individual is ineffectual. Adults become angry when
the wish to gain or to do something is thwarted. The striving and

frustration may be neurotically or realistically created. It is part of maturation to learn to accept frustration. The basic configuration of a stimulus for hostility would appear to be that a need or a wish is present; the individual's first response, if not checked by neurotic and realistic inhibitions, is to do something aggressive to meet the wish or need. If that behavior fails, hostility results and a destructive component, the affect of hostility, becomes apparent. Thus the aggressive response has as its goal the mastery of a situation. If it is ineffectual or blocked, hostility becomes manifest.

The Integrative-Adaptive Drive

In psychoanalytic formulations of human behavior one of Freud's early conceptualizations has remained unchallenged until recently. According to this concept, the responses of the infant are chaotic, attaining an organized pattern only with the development of the cortical areas of the brain and, with that, a capacity to recognize reality. With this development comes an accompanying capacity to integrate internal impulses with the demands of that reality. The failure to achieve such integration results in the psychological problems indicative of character disorders, the neuroses and the psychoses. Both the integration and the adaptation are seen as a function of the "ego," a concept that will be discussed in more detail in Chapter 9.

Even a superficial evaluation of neonatal responses does not justify the concept of the chaotic state of the neonate. He would not survive as a biological organism if the state were truly chaotic. Biological integration and adaptation characterize all living organisms. The more complex the organism, the more complex the integrative configuration and the more numerous the adaptive patterns. On a purely physiological basis, the integration of various systems of the body and the adaptation of one system to the needs and functioning of another surpass any mechanical device man has been able to construct.

More clearly related to later psychological development are the patterns of integration and adaptation that are demonstrable in the behavior of the neonate. The infant's response to hunger can again serve as an example. In satisfying this need, an integrated pattern made up of many components—rooting, moving the head toward the breast, sucking—is followed. Sucking is an inherent response which, when integrated into the total picture, results in relief of hunger.

Sucking is not learned behavior; only its efficacy for the relief of hunger is learned.

On a very simple level a capacity for adaptation is also evident in this nutrient seeking and receiving pattern of behavior. A neonate adapts to bottle feeding without the above sequence occurring. For example, the trigger area that causes a reflex response of turning the head is usually not stimulated in bottle feeding. The nipple of the bottle is often inserted into the infant's mouth as the mouth opens to emit a cry. The bottle nipple and the bottle itself are very inadequate reproductions of the human breast. The only point of similarity is that sucking the nipple provides fluid, yet the neonate adapts easily to this unbiological situation.

Another example of adaptation is the physiological acceptance by the neonate of the idiosyncracies of "scientific" adults when rigid feeding schedules are imposed. The infant adapts, usually with surprising rapidity. Few adults would have the capacity to adapt psychologically to an experience that is as alien to his total gestalt as is the rigid feeding schedule alien to the neonate's physiological rhythm.

As the human organism matures and as the neurological development institutes new demands and new capacities for adaptation and integration, both adaptation and integration become more complex. Cortical development with the accompanying capacity for recall and reasoning become an important part of the individual's integrative and adaptive capacity, but those manifestations are only a refinement of an inherent capacity. They become the psychological components of the integrative-adaptive drive. Once the specifically psychological response of the individual becomes manifest, this integrative-adaptive response is referred to as the "ego."

[7]

Energy

THE LIFE PROCESS cannot be defined without some reference to "energy," its utilization and its replenishment. All functioning of a living organism involves greater or lesser expenditures of energy. The nature of the original source of energy as an entity, irrespective of the form it takes, has yet to be fully understood, but there is some knowledge of the manner in which energy becomes available for physical utilization by the human organism.

The question of the source of psychic energy is proving to be more baffling and controversial than that of the source of physical energy. There has been a tendency to modify the term energy with a descriptive adjective. This custom, whether by intent or by accident, has resulted in conceptualizing that particular form of energy as specific and not related to the general energy reservoir of the organism. Perhaps the most familiar example of this tendency is observed in writings about Freudian psychology where there are frequent references to libidinal energy and aggressive energy. It is suggested there that the specific type of energy becoming delibidinized or deaggressified through modification thus becomes available for other psychic processes more distantly related to the original psychic activity.

In contrast to this theory, consider the following example. If a person has played golf to the point of overwhelming fatigue and is too tired to read a book but wishes to sleep instead, it is not suggested that his intellectual energy has been deintellectualized and placed at the call of his muscular demands. Rather, it is said that the golf game has utilized all of the stored energy he has available and thus exhaustion has occurred.

There is another significant implication of this example. A businessman may join his friends for a game of golf on the day he is struggling with a momentous problem in his work. He plays a poor game and realizes something is wrong. He says that his mind is not on

81

the game. Or he may force himself to pay attention to his game in order to forget his business worries; he puts his all into the game with surprising success. Whichever way his energy flows, it is not entirely at his beck and call. Regardless of what happens, it is not said that his motor energy is demotorized in the service of his intellect, or vice versa. Rather, it is said that more energy is diverted to one activity at the price of less energy being available for another.

The Energy Reservoir

A conceptualization of energy as specific in nature rather than convertible to specific uses would appear to be not only unnecessary but contrary to current theories. At present, energy is considered to be a nonspecific force utilizable in specific form, whether it is electrical, thermal, physical, or psychic in nature. Energy and the capacity of living cells to utilize energy are essential characteristics of life. But it is the nonspecificity of the energy reservoir, subject to specific utilization, that makes life possible. The source of energy is biological.

This concept of energy is not completely satisfactory, however, unless another aspect of the living organism is introduced as a corollary. By some mechanism not yet fully understood the healthy organism tends to utilize energy to maintain a minimal if not optimal functioning of all its essential parts before energy becomes available for the more effective functioning of one particular part. This use of energy is perhaps most succinctly demonstrated in the body's autonomic system. The energy required for the heart to beat so that an adequate circulation of blood is maintained to provide the required oxygen for the metabolic processes of the body remains available even when the energy reservoir is depleted. The physical fatigue of the runner, for example, requires him to cease his activity, but his heart does not stop beating.

Undoubtedly there are inherent differences in human beings that partially determine the utilization of energy beyond the minimal amount required for the maintenance of life. As indicated in Chapter 5, some neonates appear to utilize energy in motor activity in excess of body needs. Individual differences are even more discernible in later life when intellectual processes also become involved. In part the shift is undoubtedly the result of life experiences, but in part it is also the result of the inherent differences that determine the path of release for energy-charged needs. An individual may utilize available energy, for example, for motor or for intellectual activity. The scholar and the athlete represent opposite utilization patterns of the energy available in excess of the essential amount needed for basic maintenance of life.

In addition to this possibly inherent tendency to divert the major share of energy into one system rather than another, there is another inherent characteristic of importance in understanding the psychological significance of human behavior. There may be a variation in the basic energy endowment of individuals, a difference that in time may be found to be rooted in congenital variations of the metabolic processes. At present, there is no measurement available to ascertain what the energy potential of each person is. So, for the time being, the validity of the concept of variation in the basic energy endowment can only be empirical and the observations subject to other interpretations.

The concept of an energy reservoir in excess of basic organic needs, and the inherent tendency to divert that energy into different channels appear to be significant in understanding the effect of life experience on the individual's psychological development. Newborn infants show contrasting responses to sucking stimulation. Some suck vigorously from birth and often continue to do so even after the physiological need for food has been gratified. Others suck much less enthusiastically, even when they physiologically require food; once their physiological hunger is satisfied, they cease sucking. Within the limits of current knowledge, there are two possible explanations for the contrasting behavior, assuming that prematurity has been ruled out. The infant who sucks vigorously has either an energy endowment that provides extra energy for activity or he channels an unusual amount of his excess energy into paths leading to gratification of the sucking urge. The less enthusiastic infant has either less basic energy endowment or a weaker sucking urge and thus requires less energy to gratify it.

It is apparent in clinical work that the channeling of energy into one area of functioning depletes the energy available for other activities. This tendency is epitomized in the neurotic individual who is unable to deal effectively with nonconflictual areas of his life because the energy available for psychic functioning is being channeled to energize the conflictual areas, symptomatically revealed by the psychic illness. Reasons for channeling energy into the area of conflict will become clearer when the origin of conflict and the psychic tools available for handling it are discussed.

The concept of inherent low energy endowment is a postulate that may have clinical significance. When a patient easily shows fatigue, especially fatigue related to psychological functioning, the psychotherapist readily assumes that most of the patient's energy is being diverted into the neurotic struggle. Fatigue is a common complaint of a patient who is suffering from a neurosis. It is concluded, therefore, that the neurosis is severe, a conclusion that is clearly true at one level. The neurosis *is* severe because too great a quantity of energy is bound to the neurosis, but the assumption is not justified that this individual, when freed from his neurosis, will have the same amount of energy that another person has. He may have basically less energy available for any psychological struggle and thus the resolution of the neurosis does not mean that he will be able to master all life situations. Another psychological task, not necessarily related to the one relieved by the therapy, may result in another energy failure and a recurrence of psychological illness. Thus, failure to cure a neurosis and to prevent a subsequent breakdown in psychological functioning through psychotherapy may be explainable on grounds other than the obvious gaps in knowledge concerning the nature of psychological health, how to achieve and maintain it, and how to cure psychological ills. Failure may be explainable on the basis of the inherent capacity of the individual to maintain psychological health under the multiple pressures to which the psychological structure is exposed.

Energy and Basic Psychological Tasks

There are certain major tasks that must be mastered if psychological health is to be maintained. Energy available for psychological functioning beyond the demands of those essential tasks is, in a sense, excess energy. As mentioned earlier, an individual's energy supply is first utilized to maintain his basic functioning; in a healthy individual the excess becomes available for other uses. The significance of this phenomenon is demonstrated in physical illness. During illness the essential functions of the body, particularly the heart and respiratory activities, have high priority in the determination of the use of available energy. The curative resources of the body also have priority, energy being available, for example, for the production of new cells to fight bacterial invasion or to correct the damage from trauma. The effect of the illness may decrease the efficiency of the metabolic processes that convert energy into a form usable by the body's system. As a result, the energy required for normal activities is not available. The individual is relatively weak; he can move, though with less facility and greater exhaustion. A minimal amount of energy is available for a weak performance of the usually adequately energized act.

A comparable situation exists in the interrelationship between the energy that has been converted into psychic energy and the psychological functioning of the individual. Broadly speaking, the relatively psychologically healthy individual possesses energy in excess of that required to achieve the basic psychological tasks. Excess energy is available for less primary tasks, such as abstract thought, learning, and writing books. For example, an individual is dealing with four psychologically basic tasks, none of which requires one-fourth of the total psychological energy available; the result would be that he would have free energy available for nonbasic psychological activity.

In another instance, given the same four basic tasks, one of the tasks requires the use of more than one-fourth of the reservoir of energy. In such an event, there is no excess energy available and the result is not illness but a constriction of psychic activities. Such a condition may exist, for example, when an individual is preoccupied with a major worry. Most of his otherwise excess energy will be utilized in attempting to master the worry.

There is another possibility. The individual is able to deal with the four basic psychological tasks, but an additional one is imposed on him, which he does not have the energy to meet. Several different outcomes are possible. Energy may be withdrawn from one of the basic tasks. This is only relatively possible to do in actuality, although the attempt to do so is often made, as illustrated in the defensive mechanism of denial. More typical of the effect of an additional task is the withdrawal of some of the energy utilized in mastering other tasks; the mastery of these tasks becomes less effectual and the new task is only partly mastered. Yet another possibility is the excessive withdrawal of energy from other tasks, for use in mastering the new task. Such an event may result in severe psychological disintegration.

As has been indicated earlier, the ratio between the energy required and the energy available is determined by the psychological tasks to be mastered, the complexity of those tasks and hence the energy required for mastering them, and the amount of energy available. The last factor is governed in part by nonpsychological conditions. For example, an ill person has less energy available than a well person; and a fatigued person has partially drained his energy reservoir. Also, the reservoir of available energy may be determined by an inherent energy potential which varies from individual to individual and which may be greater or less than that required for the usual tasks of psychological life.

In conclusion, there are many aspects of human psychology to be explored. A microscopic or segmented study of any one aspect is meaningless unless the findings are ultimately related to the human psychological structure as a whole. Energy is only one part of the explanation of the psychological or physical functioning of an individual, but human functioning cannot be fully understood if the energy component is ignored.

[8]

Certain Basic
Psychological Concepts

BASIC TO THE CONCEPTS formulated by Freud is the hypothesis that there is an unconscious and a conscious part of the psychic gestalt. Consciousness encompasses all of that of which an individual is aware at any moment. This awareness may involve thought processes, feelings, identification of objects that stimulate sensory endings, identification of internal sensations, and identification of the interrelatedness of these various components.

Probably one can be conscious of only one thing at a time. One is, however, over a relatively short span of time, conscious of many things that may be related or may be unrelated: a toothache, for example, along with a need to respond to a question someone has asked, and a wish that the day's work was over. Probably such a variety of unintegrated, unrelated ideas become conscious with such a rapidity of oscillation that they are experienced as if they occurred simultaneously. To the degree, however, that one idea demands attention, the other is ignored. Thus, a deep interest in the question to be answered may momentarily cause the toothache to be "forgotten," or, alternatively, the toothache may be so severe that the question cannot be given attention. The stimulus that suffers such vicissitudes may be of an affective nature. One "forgets" sorrow briefly if a pleasurable stimulus is sufficiently strong. One is conscious of the stimulus that has the greatest impact and the greatest cathexis, and the other stimuli are at least temporarily blocked out if their intensity and cathexis are of a lesser degree. Thus, when multiple stimuli are present (the constant state, at least during waking hours), those stimuli are filtered and integrated that have the greatest intensity or an associative relationship to other stimuli.

Stimuli are particularly significant if they can be integrated with other stimuli to provide a whole. This latter aspect is meaningful in the learning process. For example, reading a sentence covering an obscure idea requires careful scrutiny of each word. But, in addition

87

to scrutiny of each word, each word must be defined through association with previous experiences with the meaning of the word, and then it must be associated with the words that precede and follow it in the text. As each stimulating association gives meaning to a word, and as the meaning of each word becomes associated with the meaning of the previous word, the sentence is "understood." The reader becomes conscious of the meaning of the sentence; an idea has been grasped. It cannot be said, however, that the complicated process that resulted in a conscious idea was arrived at consciously. Many of the steps in defining the word and its relationship to the other words were not conscious processes. On the whole, one is conscious primarily of those stimuli that can be integrated into a conceptualization. Consciousness is thus dependent on one aspect of the unconscious, that part which can become conscious but which functions effectively even if it remains unconscious.

The Mnemic Systems

This unconscious, however, is different from certain other aspects of the concept of the unconscious. It is that part of the psychic structure to which Freud refers as the mnemic systems.[1] The mnemic system is the result of memory traces that are available for interrelation and transformation into consciousness or are repressed and thus permanently unconscious, depending on their acceptability or unacceptability if recalled. Freud comments that "We are probably inclined greatly to overestimate the conscious character of intellectual and artistic productions." This he concludes after stating, "Everything conscious has an unconscious preliminary stage; whereas what is unconscious may remain at that stage and nevertheless claim to be regarded as having the full value of a psychical process. The unconscious is the true psychological reality."[2]

In common language "unconscious" has become synonymous with the typological conceptualization that Freud first introduced but later partially abandoned.[3] However, as a conceptualization of mental processes it has value. He recognized two types of unconscious

---

1. Sigmund Freud, "The Interpretation of Dreams," *The Standard Edition of the Complete Psychological Works of Sigmund Freud,* vol. 5 (London: Hogarth Press, 1964).
2. *Ibid.*
3. Sigmund Freud, *New Introductory Lectures on Psychoanalysis* (New York: W. W. Norton, 1933).

phenomena; both of which are unconscious in the sense of the individual being unaware of them *at the moment.* One type is, however, capable of being brought to awareness; the other is not. For the latter he utilized the term "system unconscious" (Ucs). Those memories, affects, and drives that were inadmissible to consciousness were a part of the system Ucs. Those ideas and affects that are unconscious but could be brought to consciousness he attributed to the system "preconscious" (Pcs). When something was conscious it was a part of the system "conscious" (Cs).

Between the system Ucs and the system Pcs Freud recognized that there was a block which prevented that which was unconscious from becoming conscious. He states, "A psychological act goes through two phases as regards its state, between which is interposed a kind of testing (censorship). In the first phase the psychological act is unconscious and belongs to the system Ucs; if on testing it is rejected by the censorship, it is not allowed to pass into the second phase; it is then said to be repressed and must remain unconscious. If however it passes this testing it enters the second phase and thenceforth belongs to the second system which we will call the system Cs."[4]

Primary and Secondary Processes

To understand psychoanalytic references to the unconscious, another concept is important; that of the primary process and the secondary process. The primary process is characteristic of the system Ucs. In this system, Freud points out, there is no negation, no doubt, no degree of certainty, no reality consideration, and no time concept.[5] In the unconscious there are only contents, cathected with greater or lesser strength—the cathectic intensities (in the Ucs) are more mobile. The primary process results in displacement and condensation, permitting the instinctual impulses to exist together without being influenced by one another and, because of this, they are exempt from mutual contradictions. In contrast, the systems Pcs and Cs are characterized by a secondary process. It is the system Pcs that makes communication possible between different content so that ideas can influence one another and give them a place in time. Thus, the Pcs

4. Sigmund Freud, "The Unconscious," *The Standard Edition of the Complete Psychological Works of Sigmund Freud,* vol. 14 (London: Hogarth Press, 1964), p. 173.
5. Sigmund Freud, "The Special Characteristics of the System Ucs," *Ibid.,* p. 186.

carries the function of conscious, logical thought processes and of adaptation to reality.

In spite of the confusion that develops when approaching the question of an unconscious meta—psychologically, that the concept of an unconscious part of the psyche is valid—it appears demonstrable through hypnosis, through slips of the tongue, through dreams, and through some of the naive remarks of children whose awareness of the significance of their thoughts is so limited that they do not have to repress the thoughts but can verbalize them. The associations that are a part of the psychoanalytic technique equally suggest the existence of an unconscious, as do the verbalizations of a psychotic patient.

Whether that aspect of the unconscious that is not, under ordinary conditions, subject to voluntary recall is expressed as directly in the ways mentioned above can be questioned without the question being answerable. By definition, unconscious material may be present that does not become conscious and therefore its existence is unknown.

The neonate is "unconscious" in the sense that his reactions are primarily of a reflex nature and are in direct response to stimulation without awareness being involved. This is not the result of psychic mechanisms of repression but the biological state of neurological immaturity. With the development of the neurological system conscious awareness evolves, but that conscious awareness encompasses only certain areas. The individual, for example, remains unconscious of the functioning of the gastrointestinal tract, becoming aware of it only when pain or other discomfort results because of its malfunctioning. Thus, consciousness encompasses a limited area of the function of the total organism, is a small part of the total psychic structure, and is a special development from the unconscious format of the primary organic structure. Consciousness is the result of the development of associative pathways beyond the direct reflex response between sensory stimulation and motor discharge. These associative pathways result in the conversion of memory traces into thought processes that define that of which we say we are conscious.

The Ego and the Id

In 1923, Freud divided the psychic structure by lines drawn through a somewhat different but overlapping plane than he did in his discussion of the conscious and the unconscious aspects of thought processes.[6] In this writing he formulated the concept of the id, the ego, and the superego. The id is unconscious. "It contains everything that is inherited, that is present at birth, that is laid down in the constitution—above all, therefore, the instincts which originate from the somatic organization and which find a first psychical expression [here] in the id in forms unknown to us."[7] The id is characterized by its utilization of primary process mechanisms. It is not only unconscious, but perhaps could be utilized as the equivalent of the previous concept of the system Ucs. The id is never consciously known. Only its derivatives can be recognized.

The ego, in contrast, functions according to the secondary process. Secondary process mechanisms are based upon rational and logical thought and are in response to and conditioned by reality. The ego is more closely related to the systems Pcs and Cs. That this is not a satisfactory equation of two different conceptualizations of the psychic structure will be discussed in the next chapter.

When id impulses can be discharged, the ego and id cannot be differentiated. When id impulses press for discharge and the ego resists this discharge, the nature of the impulses can be postulated. In dreams, but particularly in the behavior, verbalizations, and fantasies of psychotic patients, the most direct manifestations of id impulses are observed. Even in the latter, however, some distortion disguises the id impulses sufficiently so that the actual roots still remain somewhat obscure.

6. Sigmund Freud, "An Outline of Psycho-Analysis," *The Standard Edition of the Complete Psychological Works of Sigmund Freud,* vol. 23 (London: Hogarth Press, 1964), p. 145.
7. *Ibid.*

[9]

The Ego

ALTHOUGH A GREAT DEAL HAS been written about the ego, many conceptually unintegrated components of our knowledge of it persist. Part of the difficulty is a matter of definition. Freud points out that, with the development of recognition of the external world, internal impulses become modified in their expression. This modification Freud attributed to the ego.[1] He also states, "Under the influence of the real external world which surrounds us, one portion of the id has undergone a special development. From what was *originally a cortical layer* [italics added], provided with organs for receiving stimuli and with apparent protection against excessive stimulation, a special organization has arisen which henceforward acts as an intermediary between the id and the external world. This region of our mental life has been given the name of ego."[2] The ego thus represented "what may be called reason and common sense, in contrast to the id which contains the passions." Finally, through the influence of the parents and the child's identification with the parents, a "precipitate of the ego" forms, the ego ideal and the superego. This development results in another intermediary role for the ego, namely, between the id, reality, and the superego.[3]

The id represents the primitive instinctual structure. The id is completely asocial, amoral, and without ethical concepts. It demands gratification of inherent needs regardless of the price the external world must pay. The superego, which will be more fully discussed in Chapter 13, provides a check on the impulses of the id in order to facilitate maximum gratification in a social world. It is a tool by

1. Sigmund Freud, "An Outline of Psycho-Analysis," *The Standard Edition of the Complete Psychological Works of Sigmund Freud,* vol. 23 (London: Hogarth Press, 1964), p. 144.
2. Sigmund Freud, "The Mind and Its Workings—The Psychical Apparatus," *Ibid.,* p. 145.
3. Sigmund Freud, "The Ego and the Id," *Ibid.,* p. 25.

means of which the individual attempts to live as a cog, instead of as a pivot, in that world.

The capacity of the individual to define reality and the requirement that he obey his own superego results in the ego serving an organizing function, thereby enabling the impulses, if possible, to be expressed in the framework of reality and in harmony with the standards of the superego. Because reality may not permit such discharge or may not provide means for the discharge, or because the superego may forbid it, the ego's task becomes one of controlling the discharge of primary impulses under such circumstances, either by modifying the form of discharge to make it acceptable where it was previously unacceptable or by preventing its discharge.

The function of the ego as a mediator between the id, the superego, and the reality world raises the question as to whether the ego is a part of the system Cs, Pcs, or Ucs. Freud indicates that the ego is primarily part of Pcs or Cs, but he also suggests that it is, in part, unconscious. The last, to be consistent with previous formulations, would seem essential, but its unconsciousness would also have to be part of the system Ucs because it is questionable whether certain aspects of the ego's functioning could ever come into consciousness. To mediate, that which is to be mediated must be known. Because the id impulses are unconscious and cannot, unless they can pass the censor, become part of the system Pcs or Cs and because the ego would appear to function as the censor and bar this passage of unacceptable impulses, the ego in that function must itself be a part of the system Ucs. Many aspects of the ego, however, are conscious—certainly that part which is manifested by rational thought processes. The possibility of it being part of the system Ucs, however, produces a new dilemma. If it is so, it should function according to the primary process, a direct antithesis of what is usually considered its function. In fact, in the early conceptualization of the ego, the secondary process was an inherent function. If the ego is a part of the system Ucs, it must retain its secondary process functioning. Another possibility is that there is an intermediate area between the Ucs and Pcs which is an area of interchangeability between the permanently unconscious and that which can be recalled. The important concept, however, is that none of these systems are as sharply differentiated as implied earlier.

In its organizing function the ego not only bars id impulses from expression, but also relegates to the unconscious experiences and affective responses that for some cause arouse neurotic anxiety.

What is refused admission to consciousness or is repressed and becomes thereby unconscious does not disappear but remains in the unconscious, at times threatening to bypass the censor by direct escape or indirectly by a modification in form. Slips of the tongue are an example of an unconscious reaction evading the censor. The effectiveness of the censor is weakened under many conditions. Fatigue, sleep, alcohol, toxicity, and overtaxation of the ego are some of the conditions under which the vigilance of the censor is less efficient.

The study of the function of the ego as an intermediary and as an organizer of the total psychic structure led to further study of the conflicts with which the individual struggles, and also to a study of the way in which the ego deals, or attempts to deal, with those conflicts. Thus, the defense mechanisms of the ego came under scrutiny. For a time this specific function of the ego became of primary interest in the exploration of the psychic structure because of the important part it played in the personality configuration and symptomatology that develops as a result of conflicts, those configurations and symptoms being a manifestation of the ego's attempt to handle the conflicts.

The ego cannot function as representative of "reason and sanity" until the development of perception and the conceptualization of reality. Freud states, "The id is the older of the two; the ego has developed out of it like a cortical layer, through the influence of the external world."[4] This implication of the later development of the ego from reality perception was not, however, Freud's only concept of it. Elsewhere he states that, "Even before the ego exists, its subsequent lines of development, tendencies and reactions are already determined."[5] He attributed this to hereditary factors.

Others explain the development of the ego somewhat differently. They suggest that in the developmental sequence the id, instead of predating the ego, develops synchronously, with the development of the ego from an undifferentiated state of the ego-id. Willie Hoffer suggests that at least the anlage of the ego is inherent in the organism. He states, "Except for the experience of birth, the infant is equipped with the means of achieving equilibrium between his inner

4. Sigmund Freud, "Moses and Monotheism," *The Standard Edition of the Complete Psychological Works of Sigmund Freud,* vol. 23 (London: Hogarth Press, 1937), p. 96.
5. Sigmund Freud, "Analysis Terminable and Interminable," *International Journal of Psychoanalysis* 18 (1937).

needs without leading necessarily to traumatization."[6] This, it will be recalled, Phyllis Greenacre indicates occurs in intrauterine development because the motor discharge potential develops ahead of the sensory response and thus tension does not mount.[7]

As indicated earlier, Freud's stress on the function of the ego as an intermediary and as an organizer brought to light its function in terms of adaptation to reality, integration of the multiple internal impulses demanding discharge and the demands of the superego. Heinz Hartmann points out that the conflicts, while playing a significant part in the growth of the ego, are not the only roots of its development. He states, "Not every adaptation to the environment or every learning and maturation process is a conflict. I refer to the development *outside of conflict* of perception, intention, object comprehension, thinking, language, recall-phenomena, productivity, to the well-known phases of motor development, grasping, crawling, walking, and to the maturation and learning processes implicit in all these and many others."[8] This definition of the ego broadens its meaning and is in accordance with Freud's definition when he says, "We recognize in human beings a mental organization which is interpolated between their sensory stimuli and the perception of their somatic needs on the one hand and their motor acts on the other, and which mediates between them for a particular purpose. We call this organization their Ich [ego]."[9] This definition does not necessarily imply conflict. Only the term "mediate" implies that if there is conflict, the ego serves as mediator. Thus, if the sensory stimulation is the sight of a piece of candy, the viewer is hungry, reaches for the candy, picks it up, and eats it; this, according to the above definition, would be a manifestation of ego functioning in which there is no conflict.

Hartmann, in bringing into focus these other aspects of ego functioning refers to the "conflict-free ego sphere," using the term to denote "that ensemble of functions which at any given time exert their effects outside the region of mental conflict." He says: "I do not

6. Willie Hoffer, "Development of the Body Ego," *The Psychoanalytic Study of the Child,* vol. 5 (New York: International Universities Press, 1950), p. 22.
7. Phyllis Greenacre, *Trauma, Growth and Personality* (New York: W. W. Norton, 1952), p. 8.
8. Heinz Hartmann, *Ego Psychology and the Problem of Adaptation* (New York: International Universities Press, 1958), p. 8.
9. Sigmund Freud, "The Question of Lay Analysis," *The Standard Edition of the Complete Psychological Works of Sigmund Freud* (London: Hogarth Press, 1959), p. 194.

want to be misunderstood: I am not speaking of a province of the mind, the development of which is in principle immune to conflicts, but rather of processes *in-so-far* as, in an individual, they remain empirically outside of the sphere of mental conflict."[10] For example, a child learns that a radiator is hot. Having learned this fact, he is not ordinarily in conflict as to whether to touch it; he does not. His behavior is the result of the functioning of the conflict-free sphere of the ego. If, however, he has been forbidden to touch it, he wants to assert himself so he will not experience the seeming humiliation of obedience to another power, and yet he is aware of the pain that would result if he did touch it. His final behavior will be ego-determined, but it will involve the resolution of a conflict. Thus, the sphere of the ego becomes that of a conflict-bound sphere, not of a conflict-free sphere.

The Ego Span

As Hartmann formulates it, this definition of the ego relates its development more widely to the physical organism and particularly to the neurological system and its development, not only to the development of awareness of reality. The anlage of it is perhaps the neurological synapse between afferent and efferent nerves in the stimulus-discharge phenomenon of the reflex arc. With the increasing complexity of the associative pathways of the brain, the increased control of the body musculature, and finally the development of perception, the function of the ego equally becomes progressively more complex. But, as defined by Hartmann, it becomes apparent that it is, as Freud states, "interpolated between their sensory stimuli and the perception of their somatic needs, on the one hand, their motor acts on the other."[11]

Thus, described in terms of its function, the ego is manifested in the integration of various skills, both motor and intellectual, that enable the individual to determine a goal, select tools that will serve in attaining that goal, and set into motion those mechanisms that enable him to reach his goal. To return to the hungry person and the piece of candy, he is aware of hunger and aware of the piece of candy. This double awareness can be integrated with a third awareness, that the candy will allay the hunger. As a result of this integration of

10. Hartmann, *Ego Psychology and the Problem of Adaptation,* p. 8.
11. Freud, "The Question of Lay Analysis," p. 195.

three separate awarenesses, a goal is formulated: to reach the candy so it can be eaten. The person has walking skills; he integrates his goal with this skill and walks to the candy. Thus, with the utilization of other motor skills he finally attains his goal and eats the candy. His awareness of hunger, of the candy, of candy allaying hunger, and of his ability to walk would not have resulted in this behavior pattern unless the four were integrated into a unit pattern of response. This is an ego function.

Suppose, as the individual walks toward the candy, a chair is in the way and prevents him from walking in a straight line. An additional aspect of reality—the chair—has been introduced, the knowledge of which he must also integrate into his goal-directed action. He adapts to this, walking around the chair instead of walking blindly into it. This adaptation is also an ego function. This example of the role of the ego in integration and adaptation is one that illustrates, however, a high level of ego functioning and also describes *how* it functions rather than *why* it functions.

In Chapter 5 it was suggested that there may be as a part of the instinctual urge for survival, an adaptive-intergrative drive. This concept perhaps is defended as a psychoanalytic one on too-thin ice. Freud describes the id thus: "In the id there are no conflicts; contradictions and antitheses persist side by side in it unconcernedly, and are often adjusted by the formation of compromises."[12]

He also suggests that possibly there are at least some functions later attributed to the ego that are in operation earlier. He writes, "It may well be that before its sharp cleavage into an ego and an id, and before the formation of a superego, the mental apparatus makes use of different methods of defense from those which it employs after it has reached these stages of organization."[13]

The question of an inherent-adaptive drive was postulated on this slim basis and as a result of thoughts stimulated by those who are hypothesizing as inherent component of the ego. The biological patterns of integration and adaptation that serve for the survival of the organism thus become, with psychic differentiation, a psychological response. During the process of further maturation, knowledge of the external world develops and this knowledge is integrated into the

---

12. *Ibid.,* p. 196.
13. Sigmund Freud, "Inhibitions, Symptoms and Anxiety-Addenda," *The Standard Edition of the Complete Works of Sigmund Freud,* vol. 20 (London: Hogarth Press, 1964), p. 164.

developing personality. New tools for discharge of inherent drives become available; these are integrated into the patterns of response to stimuli. Affective responses are also experienced and integrated. In order to bring about integration of the increasingly complex internal and external world, adaptive mechanisms are utilized.

Without a biological pattern of integration and adaptation existing in the physical organism, the organism would not survive. The organism might take in food, but the mechanism of swallowing would not result in a stimulation of the progressive contraction of the esophagus and the food would remain in the upper part of the gastrointestinal tract. Every function of one component of the physical organism is integrated with the other parts of the organism, and is, within limits, able to adapt to different conditions and thereby carry out its primary function in spite of different conditions. Were there not an inherent pattern for integration and adaptation that becomes manifest psychologically, conflicts per se would not necessitate a solution and the individual—if he survived—would remain in a state of chaos. Clearly, such gross absence of some resolution of conflicting impulses and absence of reality adaptation would be incompatible with survival. Many clinical examples of small areas of failure of integration and adaptation do exist in every personality. The impulsive child often gives a glimpse of the chaos that exists when integration is absent.

When adaptive patterns of behavior are adequate and the internal drives can be discharged and internal needs met in a manner that is compatible with and practical in reality and is in harmony with the superego, no conflict arises. The internal and external demands and the internal and external resources are integrated and the individual experiences no continued tension. What tension is present, as a result of the pressure for discharge of internally originating impulses or internal needs, is readily discharged by the carrying out of the impulse or the gratification of the need.

When internal resources, the resources available in the external reality, and the demands of reality and the superego cannot directly or by adaptation be integrated with internal urges, a conflict is created. The internal urge presses for discharge. This creates anxiety, either because of the fear of being overpowered by the instinctual impulses, because of objective fear of the consequences if the impulse is effectively carried out, or because of fear of the superego. Anxiety serves as an alarm signal, and defense mechanisms are mobilized to protect the integrated part of the psyche.

Erogenous Zones
and Cathexis

THE PSYCHOLOGICAL MATERIAL in this book is based on certain concepts first formulated by Freud and later modified by him and by others. Among those contributions of Freud that have withstood modification without being abandoned is the concept of steps, stages in human psychological maturation. Unless extremely crippling events occur in early life, all individuals progress from one level to the next, from birth to maturity. Each of these stages of growth have specific characteristics, and specific conflicts occur in each stage. Failure to attain an adequate resolution of these conflicts or the manner in which conflicts are resolved affect the ultimate character and personality patterns of the growing child as well as of the adult.

Freud's recognition of the stages of maturation and the vicissitudes of their development was based on his observations in working with neurotic patients. Some people used this concept as evidence that the stages in themselves are preneurotic manifestations of the ultimate illness; however, neither Freud nor his followers implied this conclusion. On the contrary, psychoanalysts have assumed that these steps in maturation are characteristic of *all* human psychological growth. Psychological illness results from the failure to master each phase adequately in the course of maturation. The significance of the stages of psychological maturation lies in the fact that each stage is characterized by the dominance of a specific erogenous zone.

As was discussed in detail in Chapter 4, the first phase of psychological maturation is the oral phase. (There the author postulated an earlier nonpsychological phase for which she used the term "primary functional level of development.") The oral period is one in which the infant's primary source of pleasure is the area of the mouth. The mouth is, therefore, considered an erogenous zone. The use of the term "erogenous" rather than "erotic" is appropriate and, perhaps, at this point a definition of the term "erotic" should be interpolated. Erotic describes a particular type of pleasure experience characterized by mounting tension under stimulation, with relaxation normally occurring as a result of the response of the area of stimulation itself, the erogenous zone. The period of forepleasure, as the period of response to stimulation is described, is characterized by an anticipatory tension that leads, if external and internal conditions are favorable, not to discomfort that is intolerable but to a peak of tension and then relaxation. The state of tension is actively pleasurable (unless it cannot be resolved through the organ that is stimulated) and the state of relaxation is one of contentment. This description applies to mature sexuality, the orgasm representing the point at which tension ceases and relaxation occurs. Different but parallel experiences occur, however, especially in the immature individual.

Development of Erogenous Zones

What is the secret of the development of the erogenous zones? Under normal conditions neurological development, specifically myeliniza-tion, follows a set path from cephalic to caudal levels. Furthermore, a new neurological development results in the temporary dominance of its specific functions. An example, mentioned earlier, is the fate of sucking reflexes when chewing becomes a part of the neurological development. Although the chewing and biting of the nipple while nursing may be related to tender gums caused by the growth of teeth, it occurs in a mucosal area that is significantly eroticized. As will be clear later any sensory stimulation that does not cause pain results in the passive experience of erotic gratification. In other words, gratification is more intense because the basic pleasurable experience is transcended by more intense pleasure than the initial stimulation arouses. We do not know why this is so. It may be related to chemical changes, to the sensory effect of increased blood supply, to electrical changes, or to factors that at present are unknown.

The question can be raised as to why, if mucosal areas are those that become erogenous zones, the nose has not had a role in psychosexual development. It is possible that this is because the time in which the nose is dominant is at birth; that it is responsive at birth is indicated by the sneezing of the newborn. Nose picking has been seen as a displaced expression of various impulses. Perhaps this displacement is possible because of an imprint from very early erogenous dominance. The dominance clearly is shared with oral dominance. Dominance of the oral erogenous zone results in gratification and relief of hunger. Its specific pleasure is thus reinforced and it continues to be a source of satisfaction. On the other hand, nasal eroticism may not completely disappear. Many people, when about to sneeze, experience mounting tension. If the sneeze is aborted, there is a certain degree of frustration; if the sneeze comes, there is a certain pleasurable relaxation. When, as in severe hay fever, the paroxysms of sneezing are of such a nature that the relaxation is never fulfilled because of the immediate recurrence of the mucosal stimulation, patients describe a convulsive-like somatic response that finally ends the paroxysm.

Earlier in this chapter, the orgasm was described as the point at which tension ceases and relaxation occurs. A similar phenomenon seems to occur during the oral phase of development when the mouth is the primary erogenous zone; it is termed "oral erotism." Observations have shown that many infants suck when not hungry; however, the intensity of the sucking gradually decreases as the child falls asleep. Yet, with some, the intensity continues and then ceases with an abruptness not explainable by the depth of the level of sleep attained. Whether this tension-relaxation configuration is determined by an orgastic resolution of the tension is a question not satisfactorily answerable at the present time. Each suck may represent a response of tension peak and relaxation, with the final relaxation resulting from exhaustion of the stimulus. An alternative concept—that the entire period of sucking is preorgastic—is hard to defend in view of the infant's state of relaxation during sucking. But, with the present state of knowledge, all that can be said is that some stimulus institutes a sucking response which apparently leads to mouth sensations that result in release of tension.

The striking aspect of the phenomenon of nonhunger-stimulated sucking is that, although tension created by hunger results in crying and evidence of biological "discontent" if the tension is not relieved, the tension from the nonhunger sucking stimulation does not call forth this response. It is self-resolving through the act of sucking. It is an eroticized response characterized by stimulus-tension followed by tension resolution and relaxation, and the tension does not exceed the pleasure threshold.

The shift to the next dominant erogenous zone—the anus and the urethra—heralds the evolvement of the anal period of development. These areas become eroticized and erotic gratification is gained primarily through the expulsion and retention of excretory matter.

The third erogenous zone in the sequence of development is the penis in the boy and the clitoris in the girl, and this is the oedipal stage. That this stage has been reached is evidenced by the frequency of masturbatory behavior at this time. By the time this shift in the dominant erotic zone has occurred, the individual's psychological development is such that emotional responses are becoming fused with the sensations experienced from the eroticized body area. Because of the stage of emotional maturation, the child is now able to love. For reasons that are partially understandable, this love is turned with greater intensity toward the parent of the opposite sex.

The partial resolution of the oedipal stage of psychological maturation leads to the latency phase. During this phase there is no clearly defined erogenous zone. The chief characteristic of this phase is psychological growth in terms of reality adaptation.

The end of latency is determined to a large extent by the maturational activity of the reproductive glands. Adolescence occurs in response to the effect on the psychological structure of the secretions from these glands. During this period many parts of the body are eroticized. The resolution of this period establishes the identity of the adult. If the adult has weathered fairly adequately the progression of erogenous zones, and this progression has been paralleled by a more encompassing psychological maturation, the adult is erotically responsive on a heterosexual level. He is also psychologically mature in his response to the demands of his own internal needs and to the resources available for gratification in his environment.

Each step in maturation from one erogenous zone to the next results in the dominance of the newly eroticized area. The eroticization of the preceding zone does not, however, entirely disappear. It is less intense, but still provides a modicum of pleasure. Some might argue that this enjoyment is a neurotic perpetuation of the earlier stage; however, in view of the relative universality of the continued gratification from earlier erogenous zones, it would seem sound to assume that the significant consideration is the *degree* of dominance for erotic gratification of the latest maturational stage achieved.

Libidinal Drive

Freud based his concept of the instinctual drive, "eros," on the recognition of erogenous zones. The aim of that instinctual drive is "to establish ever greater unity and to preserve them [the erogenous zones] thus—in short bind together."[1] The energy involved in this instinctual drive he called "libido." For the most part the term *libido* is used as a synonym for eros as well as an indication of libidinal energy. In a broad sense libido can be translated as love. But, in psychoanalytic theory, libido is particularly that response initially' related to erogenous zones, later to be modified in the course of maturation and development by the biological changes occurring during growth, as well as by the life experiences of the individual.

A later discussion of the defenses and adaptive mechanisms will clarify some of the obscurities of this cursory presentation of the libido theory, but a simple example may give some substance to it. The maturation of the libidinal drive in adulthood results in the capacity to attain heterosexual orgasm. Part of the energy available for this response may be directed into other channels. This diversion may be neurotically determined in some instances, but not all such diversion is neurotic. For example, a mature person may enjoy his work, not with casual pleasure but with an intensity that results in a real emotional (libidinal) investment in it. In such an instance, some of the individual's libidinal drive has a modified goal and some of the libidinal energy is invested in attaining that goal. The instinctual drive is then sublimated, directed into a constructive channel of discharge that leads to a secondary goal rather than to the primary goal of direct sexual discharge in orgasm.

The terms "primary" and "secondary" are used frequently in this material. It is unfortunate that the term secondary in popular usage carries with it a certain depreciative connotation. That is not the meaning of the term in the context in which it is used here. Rather it refers to a structure that is built on a basic (or primary) foundation.

The libidinal drive is an aspect of most significant behavior in the sense that if a drive to attain a goal that is emotionally meaningful to the individual is not fulfilled by the individual's behavior, the resulting frustration increases tension; it is not released and it is unpleasant. If the drive is gratified by attainment of the goal, tension beyond the threshold of pleasurable excitation does not arise and the tension is relieved by the attainment of the goal. The amount of libidinal energy invested in the process of attaining the goal determines the amount of potential tension and the degree of frustration

1. Sigmund Freud, "An Outline of Psycho-Analysis," *The Standard Edition of the Complete Psychological Works of Sigmund Freud,* vol. 23 (London: Hogarth Press, 1964), p. 148.

or gratification possible. However, libidinal drive, as defined here, is not the only form of energy expended in many psychic activities.

Cathexis

If one approaches personality development solely from an evaluation of the shift in the erogenous zones and the implications this shift has for the ultimate psychological structure, a metapsychological distortion is inevitable. These changes are only a part of the psychological growth process that is occurring; they are expressed effectively in the development of new erotic zones and the shift in intensity of that eroticization. But the erogenous zones are also significant because of their relationship to a progressively more complex psychological structure.

One phenomenon of the growth of a more complex psychological structure is the individual's conceptualization of himself and of objects, and his response to both. With development, the neonate moves beyond the initial period of awareness of objects; they become emotionally meaningful to him. Because the infant-object is a unit in which the object has a functional role, the object undoubtedly is a part of the anlage of the primary narcissistic response as long as it functions and is needed. Whether this is true or not, the object assumes importance as the infant becomes capable of differentiating the self and the nonself.

Gratification of the primary narcissistic needs results in the emotional experience associated with a sense of security. Absence of that gratification creates the emotional response of a sense of insecurity. As the object is identified as providing security or failing to do so, the object becomes invested with emotional meaning to the infant and it is said that the object is "cathected."

The term "cathexis" as used in modern psychological theory is difficult to define without leading to sometimes rather absurd conclusions from a too-literal interpretation of the definition. It has been referred to, for example, as the investment of libidinal energy in the object which is cathected. Following this definition, the object is then said to be charged with libidinal energy. This, however, is true only as the object is part of the individual psychic structure through the individual's perception of the object. The object itself cannot absorb psychic energy from the person who values it. Its meaning and the image of it as experienced by the individual become charged with psychic energy.

Cathexis of an object is possible only with a certain degree of psychological maturation, when the object's function arouses an affective response. And when the functional meaning and the image of the object are fused, the object becomes a symbol of its function. An object is said to be cathected when it has a high degree of affective meaning with the result that a great deal of affective psychic energy is channeled into any response to it. An object is not cathected unless it originally had a function affectively charged and unless it has become a symbol of that function.

The function the object serves, either in reality or as a symbol, may have positive value. If so, it is said to be "positively" cathected; it is a love object. If, for example, a child has found that a cat has served to relieve many lonesome hours and has filled in many gaps in the gratification of the child's emotional needs—gaps that have occurred because of the inadequacy of the adult human beings in his environment—the cat may have become an object of intense emotional meaning to the child and, therefore, be positively cathected. If, however, the function of an object has resulted in a mobilization of protective devices, it then may be "negatively" cathected. If the cat has been a cantankerous, scratching animal that has epitomized the negatives in the child's life, it may function as a symbol of all the child resents. The child may then show an "irrational" hostility toward cats—a hostile cathexis of the object.

It should be pointed out that the above concept of hostile cathexis is in contrast to the one held by those who see cathexis as always related to the investment of libidinal energy, with the hostility manifested being a denial of the libidinal response. It would appear more valid to conceptualize cathexis as any intense emotional investment, of whatever nature, in an object that is serving or has served as a stimulus for intense affective discharge.

As soon as an object loses its functional role or its symbolic meaning loses its significance for the individual, the object is said to be "decathected." This phenomenon is most clearly seen clinically with older children or adults. To return to the example of the friendly cat, the small child, having found an answer to otherwise unmet needs, may grow into an older child to whom the possession of a cat is essential for happy living. Eventually a relationship is formed with a human adult who can gratify the needs that until then have been met only by the symbolic meaning of the cat. The symbolic object has now been replaced by a real object, and this object becomes cathected. The cat as a love object becomes decathected.

Decathexis of a transiently cathected object is seen repeatedly in infancy. The bottle, the breast, and the blanket are all familiar examples. They all serve important functions; they become love objects. In time, the infant no longer needs them and they are decathected. It is only when the infant develops a capacity for, and at the same time has a need for, the use of objects as symbolic representations that relatively permanent cathexis of the objects develops. But the early phase of object cathexis is the beginning or the precursor of the psychological capacity to experience object love.

[11]

Anal Stage
of Development

THE FIRST STAGE OF PSYCHOLOGICAL development, the oral stage, was explored in detail in an earlier chapter. This chapter continues the discussion of emotional maturation, focusing on the second stage, the anal. During the latter part of the first year of life and the early part of the second year, neurological maturation provides the infant with new ways to meet his needs. His motor skills, awareness of needs, and recognition of the sources of gratification for those needs progressively develop. His ability to utilize motor skills to attain, to hold, and to throw away those sources of gratification increases and becomes significant. The child's response to this growth is observable in many areas. Achievement of greater and more coordinated motility is interesting to follow. Before the infant is able to walk, he begins to use his capacity to control his muscles. He first reaches for an object; later, if the object is out of reach, he initiates body movements that bring him closer to it. This development leads to various patterns of motility, the most common pattern of which is crawling. Finally, his motor control is sufficiently developed to enable him to walk.

Beginning to walk offers more than one type of gratification for the child. Once he can pull himself to an upright position, he often does so with seemingly no other motivation that that of exercising his new skill. Before the child is able to walk without the support of the sides of his crib or playpen he will walk around those confined areas not necessarily to reach something but for the purpose of being uprightly mobile. His first independent steps also appear to be enjoyed as an act in themselves.

When the child walks from one person to another, his reaction is different from that observed in the playpen. He laughs and exhibits an eagerness that at first defeats him in his use of his newly acquired skill; he often falls. This behavior is in part explainable by the

107

attitude of the adults helping him. They too are eager, and by their manner and tone of voice they undoubtedly stimulate the child. The apparent eagerness of the child, however, is often greater than the companion eagerness of the adult. Not only is the mastery of walking pleasurable in itself, but that mastery serves other drives. For example, because of his new skill, the child is able to reach someone who is meaningful to him, such as his mother, who may be elsewhere in the room or house.

At the same time as walking becomes established as a means of locomotion, the child also has developed an increased capacity to sustain an interest in objects that are not close at hand. As a result of this combination of sustained interest and motor skill, he can see something at a distance, maintain an interest in attaining it, and try to reach it. He has acquired tools to prevent the frustration he previously had to accept unless others would do for him what he could not do for himself. The desire to avoid the displeasure of frustration intensifies his eagerness to use the tools.

In certain children there is an interesting side picture to this active striving for a defined goal. After taking his first solo steps the child will be selective in his mode of motility, depending on his goal. He will work hard at mastering walking if his immediate goal is simply mastery or reaching a fairly readily available object. If, however, he is very eager to reach the object, he will choose the surer method of crawling toward it. In spite of the importance of using a newly acquired skill, he is adaptive. The intensity of the internal pressures, the reality of the situation in the environment, and a response to the usefulness of his particular skills result in an integrated response that is adapted to the total configuration. His eagerness to walk becomes secondary until the immediate goal of getting somewhere surely and quickly is accomplished. This solution is an obvious one for the child; it is one example of the early evidence of an adaptive-integrative capacity in the very young child. Many adults faced with a situation of comparable magnitude are paralyzed by conflicting possibilities and do nothing, or they shift from one way of handling the situation to another, thereby confusing themselves and others!

Development of Control

At about the chronological age at which the infant develops the muscular control that makes walking possible, his neurological development enables him, with relative facility, to control the anal and urethral sphincters and thus to control his excretions.[1] Acquiring a new skill is typically gratifying in infancy, as indicated in the discussion of walking. It is probable, therefore, that progressive achievement of sphincter control is a pleasurable experience. The psychoanalytic study of older children and adults offers a convincing basis for considering this period of development as one of anal eroticization, pleasure being experienced with the sensation of with-holding and expelling feces in particular but also urine. Whether the development of sphincter control is experienced during the second year of life as erotically stimulating or whether that response gradually develops with success is speculative. That the infant's ability to control excretions is psychologically significant to later development is readily demonstrable both in terms of characterologi-cal distortions and neuroses and also in terms of positive value systems and effective maturational patterns that foster psychologi-cally healthy adaptation in adult life.

Effective control of the excretory functions provides the child with one of his first life experiences of active, relatively complete mastery. It reveals to him his own power, a power that is not dependent on his ability to mobilize activity in others. Within limits he can allow his excretions to be discharged or he can retain them according to his own whim, not according to the whims of others. The small child often evidences pleasure in the result· of this achievement. He becomes interested in his feces or urine and, with real concentration, watches the urinary stream or the lengthening of the fecal mass and its final drop into the toilet bowl. He enjoys the product of his effort, he likes the odor of his feces, and he finds their consistency a source of play material. Thus, the smearing of feces that frequently occurs even before sphincter control has developed, but particularly during the early phase of actual sphincter control, does not have the implication that it may have later. It is simply the utilization of enjoyable play material that the child has brought into being.

Toilet Training

Toilet training is an important factor in the child's development at this time, in the cultural sense. Bladder and bowel controls are

---

1. Prior to the attainment of this maturational level the infant does have some sphincter control, but it is utilized effectively only with great concentration. Examples that parents give of toilet training having been achieved before the child is able to walk are in some instances historically true, but in most instances such training was achieved only superficially.

usually considered synonymous with toilet training. This is careless thinking. Bowel and bladder controls are the result of neurological development. If the development has proceeded normally, the child can decide whether he will utilize controls or not. Toilet training is the educational program instituted by the environment that teaches the child the accepted way to use the control he has. For example, the child who hides in a corner to have a bowel movement, who sits on the toilet without results and then immediately soils or wets himself when he is removed from the toilet has bowel and bladder control. He is using it to avoid accepting the "lesson" his parent is attempting to teach.

As the cultural pattern takes advantage of this developing ability of the child to control his excretory outlets by instituting toilet training, it also creates conflicts between the parent and the child. The nucleus of these conflicts is the child's wish to be master of his own body functioning, a wish that is opposed to his wish to be secure in his relationship with his parents. The parents want to control indirectly the child's excretory functions. In a sense they ask the child to relinquish part of his own control in conformity to the demands of another. In some instances the child's acceptance of this parental dictate seems to represent to him the relinquishment of a valued power. The "negatively toilet trained" child controls his excretions so that they are put now into the parentally defined proper receptacle but only where he wishes to put them, a place chosen in part because the parent disapproves.

Everything in the parent's behavior indicates that control of the excretory functions that results in the excretions being discharged in a parent-selected place will bring approbation to the child, evidence that by this act the child effectively wins the parent's love. A failure to control his functions in this way results in disapproval, an implication that parental love is being withdrawn, and the child's security is threatened. Thus, a conflict is created between an urge to master and the need to be loved.

The child has none of the aversion toward his excretions that the adult has; he actually responds to them—particularly to his feces—as if they were a creation of his own and part of himself that should be valued. To some children, the production of feces at the behest of parents is the giving of a gift; withholding them is to deprive the parents of a gift they do not deserve. A child who passes feces in secret and then hides them may be preserving something that he sees as valuable in itself or as an essential part of him, something that he wishes to preserve rather than give to the parent, who will then destroy it.

The value of the feces as a gift is enhanced by parental reactions to them. In the parent's eagerness that the child not only be toilet trained but also have a bowel movement, it is obvious that the parent values the feces. Then comes the peculiar behavior—the parent throws the feces away by flushing the toilet. This is one reason for the typical child's interest in exploring the toilet at this time and why toys are often submitted to the same fate as the feces. The child is struggling with the abstraction of "gone" and at the same time is trying to understand a value system alien to his own. In the context of the latter implication, soiling can become a hostile gesture toward the parent. As the child recognizes the distaste the parent has for the fecal substance as opposed to the parental indication of wanting it, the child may smear feces, now not only because he enjoys smearing but also because he has learned that such behavior disturbs the parents. It is a clever acting out of a response that has much in common with the later act of sarcasm!

Urination has an additional value to the child. The warm moisture provides a sensorially pleasant experience. The parent permits, in fact encourages, the child's enjoyment of a warm bath but criticizes him for a similar experience that he provides for himself. Again a value system has to be differentiated by a child too young to conceptualize the rationale for it. He only knows that somehow a needed person expects certain differentiations, rewarding with praise if those differentiations are acted on and disapproving if they are not.

Importance of the Anal Stage

These selected aspects of the toilet training period, which are only a few of the many that have been identified by therapists working with children who have not yet solved the conflicts related to this stage of development, will perhaps indicate why this period can have permanently crippling effects on the development of the child and on the later personality configuration. It is equally, however, a period of positive importance to the child. It can provide a real experience of self-respect, accompanied by increased security in his relationship with meaningful people. If the child sees the toilet training experience as evidence of real mastery—that he not only can control his sphincters but also can do so in a fashion that, by his own act, gives him approval or disapproval from others—his confidence in himself as a master of himself is augmented. And his self-initiated behavior that results in a positive response from another increases his confidence in his own ability to win and retain the love of others who are meaningful to him.

The psychologically successful achievement of toilet training also establishes a clear-cut value system on which many later values will be structured. Because compulsive cleanliness that reaches a crippling extent has been traced back etiologically to this period does not mean that a value system that includes cleanliness is undesirable. That the symptoms of an obsessive-compulsive neurosis are in part evidence of unsuccessful resolution of anal conflicts does not mean that the core of the obsessive-compulsive pattern, stripped of a neurotic overplay, is an undesirable character pattern. It is desirable according to our cultural goals that individuals strive for cleanliness and work nonneurotically but tenaciously to attain goals for themselves. It is of equal importance that people be able to tolerate incompatible ideas in order to reach sound conclusions. The individual who is a preanal personality will act on impulse, not being aware of the arguments pro and con such behavior. The individual arrested at the anal stage of conflict may not be able to make any decision because he gives equal weight to contradictory ideas. This tendency is bound to the early conflict, "to give or not to give" feces. The mature individual examines both the "to" and the "not to," makes a choice, and acts on it. The resolution of the conflicts of the anal period is an important component of desirable traits in a personality just as the failure to attain effective resolution is a part of a neurotic constellation.

Establishing a Sense of Self during the Anal Period

At this stage of development the child establishes his own sense of being an individual through negativism. This choice of method is not necessarily chance. The parent's power to keep the child from utilizing his new-found body skills appears powerful to the child. It is not surprising, therefore, that the child, in imitation, uses negativity as evidence of power. This behavior increases his self-value in terms of those characteristics he respects in others: it is an identification with a powerful parent; it is an attempt to establish the self as opposed to a previous amorphous state of being part of another; it is a gift of love to the self that says, in effect, "Look how I can value the

'I' that is as powerful as the objects I love—my mother and father."

But negativism also frustrates the wish to be loved by an external object, the parent; the child therefore vacillates in his behavior. A trial period of negativism is given up, and the child becomes sweetly wooing, reestablishing his sense of security through stimulating a response in the parents that to him is direct evidence of parental love.

Paralleling the shift in the child from a symbiotic relationship with his mother to self as an object relating to mother as a different object is a comparable development in the mature mother. She also gradually shifts from a symbiotic relationship to an object relationship with her child. To her, the child gradually becomes more and more a separate entity, although separateness is never complete. Margaret S. Mahler and Bertram J. Gosliner indicate that the father, if he has had an earlier meaningful relationship with the child, can be quite important during the anal stage of development.[2] Even if one considers fathering and fatherliness (see Chapter 2) as not basically different from mothering and motherliness, the symbiotic-like relationship between father and child has not had the meaningfulness of that between mother and child. The father's shift from this symbiotic-like pattern to a response to the child as an object separate from himself or his wife occurs with greater ease both for him and for the child. Thus, the father becomes another love object for the child, enabling him to dilute both the intensity of his relationship with his mother and some of the danger of being engulfed by her. The father's more ready response to the child as a separate entity and the child's parallel response to the father reassure the child and strengthen his drive to establish himself as an entity rather than remaining fused with another.

The various experiences during the anal period are significant from many viewpoints, one of which is the effect they have not only on the developing sense of self but also on the emotional cathexis of the self. The child ideally learns to recognize himself as an individual as well as to love himself; thus, the self becomes cathected. This self-love, narcissistic cathexis, remains a life preserving factor throughout life. If it were not present, the individual would expose himself to destructive experiences that would either cripple him or end his life. Narcissism is a part of healthy psychological growth and psychological maturity. It is a manifestation of maladjustment only when it is

2. Margaret S. Mahler, and Bertram J. Gosliner, "Symbiotic Study of the Child," in *The Psychoanalytic Study of the Child, vol. 10* (New York: International Universities Press, 1955), p. 200.

the total gestalt of the personality. The tragedy of Narcissus was not that he loved himself but that he was incapable of loving others as well.

Resolution of the Anal Phase

The current Western culture has been referred to as an "anal" culture. The validity of this description is suggested by the predominance of compulsive-obsessive elements in many neurotic illnesses as well as by the frequency of character and personality patterns that are manifestations of inadequate resolution of the conflicts of the anal developmental period. Paralleling this clinical picture is the history of an individual's background as well as what is known of the general philosophy of child rearing at the time when many now adult patients were infants. Early and vigorous toilet training was highly recommended. Increasingly fewer adult patients have been exposed to this kind of training since the early 1930s, when vigorous toilet training methods were abandoned by many mothers and they waited for the child to train himself. This approach was superseded by a compromise between the two extremes: parents were encouraged to introduce toilet training gradually when the child began to walk—the time at which his neurological development enables him to control his sphincters with relative ease.

It can never be assumed that such changes in philosophy are completely accepted, especially by parents who perhaps proudly value the psychological scars from their own infancy. (This is not a facetious remark. Compulsive neatness is a residual of the toilet training period. Such behavior may make others uncomfortable, but the individual usually prizes it highly unless it becomes a compulsive hand-washing ritual and thus a crippling neurosis.) Overly neat parents are not likely to be casual about toilet training; they either press for it too early or, to deny the urgency they feel, they delay it too long. But it would seem that there has been sufficient vacillation in toilet training practices that some change should become manifest in clinical studies. If practices per se are dominantly significant, the findings at present are not conclusive.

Changes in toilet training practices do not imply, however, a change in the parents' total approach to the child in this developmental stage. Parents wisely require of their children progressive conformity to the overall requirements of the culture. Certain psychological tasks must be achieved for the constructive continuity of a cultural philosophy. If "cleanliness" is of value in terms of social living and avoidance of infectious diseases, it is valid to try to instill it during that stage of development in which it can most readily be rooted. The ultimate development of the personality, in terms of health and disease, is probably determined not only by the way the parents handle this maturational period but equally by the strength of the child's multiple impulses, particularly the innate strength of the integrative-adaptive drive. The basis of certain personality patterns is established with the end of the anal phase of development.

During the anal stage, the child is faced with a basic task—the establishment of confidence in himself as an individual without jeopardizing his security by alienating those who are most meaningful to him. Until he reaches a solution, he is in conflict with his wish to achieve self-identity (a narcissistically rewarding experience) and with his wish to gratify his yearning for the continued love and support of others. Life experiences that foster a reality orientation determine how he handles the conflict that is inherent in these needs and goals. If he resolves the major conflicts with relative adequacy, he does so not only by having experiences but by correctly evaluating them. Usually his experiences are such that his growing self-reliance does not alienate him from those on whom he is dependent. Rather, he is rewarded by their appreciative response.

The child has learned through his trial period of negativism that hostility toward a loved person does not destroy that person, in contrast to the result of destruction of an inanimate object such as a toy. He finds, too, that the "hostility" of a loved person does not destroy *him.* Furthermore, he can love and value another without losing all of his self-appreciative feelings. He gains a greater mastery of his own impulses; he can delay their gratification and find parentally acceptable ways to gratify them without abandoning them entirely or plunging ahead for direct gratification irrespective of the cost. He develops a tolerance for immediate frustration both because of the possibility of later gratification and because of his new capacity to weigh the discomfort of frustration against the consequences of fulfillment. His ability to comprehend reality enables him to evaluate his immediate goals; it has become a part of his cognitive armature.

Control of the excretory functions plays an important part in this growth. The child *is* master; he may either concede to the parents or defy them. There is no other area of behavior in which mastery is so complete. As was pointed out earlier, the child also comes to realize, inevitably because of the parental attitude, that body excretions not only are gifts but also are disliked articles. Withholding, controlling, or free release of excretions can have a variety of meanings, depending on what the child wishes to express and how the parents react to that expression.

All of these implications of anal eroticism, sphincter control, and toilet training are a significant component not only of the anal period per se but also of the solution the child finds to the conflicts of the anal period.

[12]

The Emerging Self

WITH THE GROWING CAPACITY to differentiate the self and the object, another psychological growth pattern becomes discernible. Now the child is responding to the awareness of the "I" that seeks to survive. Moreover, he has now developed tools within his own control that enable him to achieve an outlet for his internal urges. He is no longer completely dependent upon the opportunities provided by others.

The growth process involved is one that extends over an appreciable length of time. According to some investigators, it is a dominant process extending from roughly eighteen months to three years of age; in some children it seems to begin earlier. During this time the child is progressively leaving the symbiotic relationship with the mother and establishing himself as an individual. He begins to relate to his external environment as well as being a part of it.

Many factors foster this change. The expression of internal urges now has a discernible goal and instinctual responses have become goal-directed drives. The form the response takes is in part learned through the early memory traces laid down when instinctual needs were met as a result of certain behavior and frustrated as a result of other behavior. The child understands in a simple sense both the response and the goal the response can serve; that understanding determines the nature of the response. The capacity to understand this constellation is dependent on the child's neurological development, particularly the cerebral development.

The Aggressive Drive Toward Mastery and Self-Preservation

The aggressive drive is now expressed as an effort at mastery. Successful mastery results in clear enjoyment of the achievement.

117

Frustration arouses anger toward the frustrating object. If that fails to bring favorable results, the child makes an all-encompassing response—the temper tantrum. He struggles to master walking, he wants to feed himself, and he wants to climb up and climb down. He does not want to be in a chair for the sake of being in the chair; he wants to be in it in order to master getting into it and then getting out of it. Parents often comment that they do not always understand what the child wants; anything they do for him that he seems to want makes him cross. They fail to realize that what the child wants is to *do.* He does not want to have things done for him; his goal is the doing itself. He now has tools with which to prevent the frustrations he previously had to accept. Were it not for the limits imposed by others he would aspire to becoming a monarch of all he surveys. Because others do impose limits his monarchial potential is always threatened with destruction.

This is the stage frequently referred to as the period of "negativism" in children. They seem to react against parental authority for the sake of reacting against it rather than primarily because it is frustrating. This is also the period of "negativism" on the part of parents. So many things a child wishes to do—and that would be an expression of his progressive competence—are justifiably prohibited by the parents. The child's wish to do, the parents' fear of that doing, and, therefore, their justified or unjustified prohibition of the act often result in a battle between an irresistible force and an immovable object.

Parents often find the temper tantrum one of the child's most baffling responses. The parent feels helpless to deal constructively with the child's state. From a preliminary state of paralysis the parent moves to do something, and often that something is an attempt to discharge his own mounting tension, which has characteristics, covert or overt, that resemble those of the child's behavior. Frightened by this interchange, the parent resolves to avoid similar outbreaks on the part of the child in the future. If they are avoided by the use of wise methods the effect on the child's development will be excellent. Unfortunately, the choice of method is more often directed by parent apprehension than by parent wisdom. Then the child is not helped to deal with the situation that has led to the temper tantrum but is protected from exposure to it. To understand how to handle temper tantrums and how to prevent them, one must first understand their causes. The psychological state of the child is different according to the "type" of tantrum.

One type of temper tantrum behavior is the angry response of the frustrated child expressed in an organized way. He uses the limited means at hand for discharging the tension created by the frustration; he may throw anything within reach or slap, bite, or kick. His behavior is also an attempt to communicate to the frustrating person how unsatisfactory the situation is.

During a tantrum, the child knows what his behavior is. He knows he is destroying toys or knicknacks, or that he is scarring his mother's shins, but the value of the attacked object is minimal compared to the urgent need to release the unbearable tension created by the frustration. If the child is old enough to use language as one outlet of tension, his remarks are coherent, even if illogical and distressing. He calls his opponents names, says he hates them, that he does not care, that he wishes the responsible people dead. To verbal admonishments or advice he answers impolitely but expressively, "Shut up." He is like the person who puts out a threatening fire with a new, expensive blanket. Whether the blanket is burned is not of importance at that point. A few moments of evaluating the situation might indicate other fire-extinguishing instruments, but the tension of the moment does not invite such evaluative behavior. Having responded in this emergency way, the adult questioned later as to why he did not do something different will answer, "I just didn't think of it. I took the first thing available." In this type of temper tantrum the child will become cooperative if it is possible to get his attention and if it is possible to remove the frustration, either by permitting the activity that was forbidden or by offering substitute gratification.

It is perhaps important to interpolate a little parental guidance at this point. Consistency, if it is wise, is important in parental behavior. Schematizing a sequence will perhaps indicate why sometimes superficial inconsistency is basically consistency.

Johnny, six years old, asks his mother if he can play with Tommy, who is playing outdoors on a rainy, cold day. Johnny is susceptible to colds and the doctor has advised that he not play outdoors on such a day. So, Johnny's mother says "No" and Johnny has a temper tantrum. In the course of his diatribe it becomes clear that Johnny meant (or now means) that Tommy should come into the house to play. The mother can then agree without losing her pattern of consistency. All she does in agreeing is respond to the facts rather than to her earlier ignorance of them. If, however, Johnny has a cold and, for Tommy's sake, the children should be kept separated, she may hold to her answer, "No," but not merely for the sake of being consistent. The solution of the temper tantrum may be for her to provide substitute gratification, perhaps by stopping her work and being a playmate for Johnny for a while.

Another response to frustration seen in the young child is of quite a different order. It is not the goal-directed behavior of the angry child described in the preceding paragraphs. In this instance, the child's response is not one primarily of tension discharge, it is a total response resembling the response of the neonate when biological needs are not met. The child's psychological organization is temporarily not operating and, overwhelmed by tension, he reverts to the pattern characteristic of the primary functional level of response to excess tension. Because he has greater motor control, is larger than the neonate, and has more power in his muscles, he superficially—but only superficially—appears different. The total nature of the response is fundamentally the same. It is for this reason that the child cannot be reached by reasoning during such an episode. His more mature levels of response are in abeyance and are not at the service of his psychological needs. Two conditions bring the "seizure" to an end, either exhaustion for the child or, in some cases, a soothing, cutaneous or auditory stimulus of the kind that quiets the neonate. A soothing voice expressing nonsense syllables will do what real words fail completely to accomplish.

The second type of response described above occurs only when the child's tolerance for frustration has been exceeded, and he has no purposefully chosen discharge channels available. An insecure child may be more prone to this type of response because his tolerance for frustration has not been built up by the confidence that potentially frustrating situations will not prove to be actually frustrating. The secure child is less likely to have such a response because past experiences give him confidence; this particular frustration is experienced as unique, and he is aware that it will not spread indiscriminately into other areas of his wishes.

The degree of the frustration tension is also affected by the strength of the wish that is frustrated. It is not always easy to evaluate the intensity of the wish the child has, or why the fulfillment of the wish at that point is so important. The child just beginning to walk frequently falls and cries. Sometimes the cry is a response to painful injury; however, if the child is in a padded playpen or on a soft carpet, it is unlikely that the fall really caused pain. Furthermore, the nature of the crying may be quite atypical of the child's usual cry when injured. In such instances the chances are that the child is reacting massively at a primary functional level to the frustration caused by his failure to achieve an upright walking position. Another example is that of the infant when he first learns to pull himself up into a standing position in the crib. Getting down is mastered later. The infant wishing to get down but unable to do so cries. But if he is helped down he immediately pulls himself up again only to repeat the procedure. When he fails, he appears to be angry or frightened (however we wish to translate his behavior into our more experienced feelings) but the feelings are manifested because he cannot master the act of getting down. He cannot tell us what he is feeling, but his behavior appears to be a response to frustration.

At times a third factor enters into the picture of the temper tantrum, causing psychosomatic disorder. Fatigue, malaise, or hunger will reduce anyone's tolerance for frustration, but the child is more prone to temper outbreaks as a response. Furthermore, a vicious circle is thereby established when, superimposed on those discomforts that are of physical origin, frustration beyond tolerance at that point is added. The tension consumes energy, thereby increasing fatigue and causing the malaise to be less tolerable. The result may be somatic symptoms of vomiting, abdominal pain, or headaches, to give a few examples. These symptoms do not necessarily have a symbolic meaning; rather they are primarily a psychosomatic response.

These examples are offered not only as descriptive of the anal stage of development but also as an attempt to offer a clinical confirmation of the concepts expressed in Chapter 6. The aggressive drive is a drive to master; its destructive component is not nuclear in nature but is a response to the frustration of that drive. Rather than being a destructive drive from which the teeth are extracted or a drive that must lose its primary goal, in this text it is considered a drive for self-preservation. The immature response to frustration of this drive is massive goalless discharge; with further maturational development the response to frustration becomes hostility, from which stem destructive manifestations. The destructive component may, under certain conditions, have positive value. Valid destruction, as in the destruction of noxious bacteria, is an effective way of expressing the aggressive drive to master, but that occurs at a high level of abstraction. It is not the primary outlet for the aggressive drive. If the destruction is valid, what is sublimated is the hostility resulting from primary frustration of the aggressive drive, not the aggressive drive per se.

The Relationship of the Aggressive and Integrative-Adaptive Drives

In addition to the easily recognized behavior patterns having their basis in the child's aggressive strivings, the integrative-adaptive urge becomes definable as a goal-directed impulse. As a child becomes able to identify objects, he becomes occupied with exploring them. He explores his own body and he explores other objects. One of the end identification of objects—the evolvement of the recognition of self as separate from the object—is a learning experience, but the learning results from integrating a variety of experiences into a perception of the object. Out of this integrated learning, adaptive patterns begin to form. As the infant begins to crawl he does not crawl head-on into a wall; he adapts his movements so that he will not do so. This very simple form of integration-adaptation is the anlage for the complex patterns of later psychological responses.

The interrelationship of the aggressive drive and the adaptive drive becomes apparent in learning. The unknown or not understood is by definition unmastered, and an uncomfortable situation is created. Relief from the discomfort can be attained by aggressive exploration, with mastery becoming possible if knowledge is gained. Curiosity represents an aggressive attempt to master that which is mastered only by knowing. Having learned what something is, however, the individual is not comfortable until that knowledge becomes a part of his total gestalt to which he can adapt his behavior. To give a simple example, a small child, if given a toy, will be uneasy and tentative in his approach until he has explored it. He finds that it makes certain pleasurable noises and also hurts him if he hits his head with it. He ceases hitting his head in order to make the noise, but usually he does not permanently discard the toy because it did hurt his head. He learns to shake the toy in such a fashion that it does not hit his head. Having explored the toy "aggressively," he thus integrates the resultant experiences and adapts his motor responses to gain a positive experience from the toy and avoid a negative one.

During this time primary narcissism is slowly modified. With the growing capacity for emotional response the self as well as objects becomes cathected in response to experiences not so closely related to survival as is primary narcissism. The self becomes a "loved" object imbued with a feeling of self-confidence and self-esteem. The child's wish to be loved and his urge to seek love are in part directed toward himself; he is both the loving and the loved person.

During this period the child is in conflict between the impulse to remain in the symbiotic relationship and to be and act separately. This struggle to establish a free self is not without anxiety; the urge to be loved by others than the self causes a reluctance to break the earlier mutual, symbiotic pattern. The child is not yet confident that the mother's love responses will change in accordance with his own growth so that he can be secure in that fundamental relationship without giving up his strivings to become a self. It is not a philosophical struggle for him; it is a conflict founded on what he experiences, which he can respond to only on the basis of cause and effect observations. Many of his exploratory moves are met by criticism, prohibitions, and punishments. This parental behavior is in contrast to the loving behavior he knew when he was more dependent. To the child, such parental behavior is unloving behavior, and the cause-effect sequence is clear. Acting independently, carrying out his impulses, and utilizing his own skills result in loss of love. His urge for aggressive mastery is in conflict with his urge to turn to others for gratification of the wish to be loved. These conflicting wishes cannot be integrated immediately, nor can a pattern of adaptation be established without abandoning one of the wishes. This is manifestly the prototype of many later conflicts.

Security and Insecurity

Experiences that assure survival and confirm the value of the aggressive drive for self-preservation lead ultimately to a sense of security. This sense originates in the experiences of a tension-free state, but is a maturational phenomenon more encompassing than the relaxation of the moment experienced during the neonatal period. Not only is relief of tension experienced, but there also is an anticipation that relief will be provided. Thus, a sense of security implies confidence that not only an immediate stress but also future stresses will be relieved.

If, instead of a feeling of security evolving, the memory traces laid down during neonatal life offer little basis for predictable anticipation of relief from tension, a sense of insecurity results. With maturation the threat to survival is affectively experienced as anxiety. This anxiety is a primary form, having its roots at a biological level of development.

As the infant becomes increasingly aware of the external world as separate from himself, he develops trust in his milieu; he becomes confident that he can find gratification for his needs in the external world and thus gain a sense of security. Insecurity results from inadequate protection from external dangers or inadequate relief from internal discomfort through the ministrations of the external world on which he is dependent. The biological tension, resulting from inadequate care or undue alarm-stimulating events during the neonatal period, provides the foundation for a lack of confidence in the external world and a resultant type of primitive fear unrelated to reality. The infant anticipates lack of protection; he fails to develop confidence in a positive experience with the external world.

A sense of security with the accompanying confidence and trust, and of insecurity with the accompanying lack of confidence and anxiety, are demonstrable at all levels of psychological development. During the anal stage of development the child's sense of security or insecurity is partially responsible for the extent to which he uses the widened opportunities made possible by his increased motility. If he is a secure child, he feels free to explore the external world and can evaluate some of his negative experiences with it in the context of reality. For example, as he has progressively explored his environment, touching has not usually resulted in a painful experience. If he then touches a hot radiator and experiences pain, he is able to recognize that touching a radiator is different from other experiences he has had. He learns not to touch a radiator but remains confident that other parts of his surroundings are safe to touch. In contrast, an insecure child will see the experience with the radiator as a confirmation of his basic anxiety, a reaffirmation that it is not safe to touch objects. He only tentatively accepts his opportunity for experiences, even with familiar things, because he has no trust. He approaches the new with the assumption that it is dangerous unless proven to the contrary.

The roles played by security and insecurity, particularly during the second year of life, create an interesting and often disturbing confusion in evaluating a child's behavior. As an optimally secure child becomes more mobile, he will require closer supervision for a period than will an insecure child, but he will learn to discriminate between safe and unsafe situations much more readily. As a secure child first develops sufficient motor skill, he will climb precariously or explore both safe and unsafe objects indiscriminately. With mildly painful consequences, however, his discriminatory ability begins to control his behavior. While he is developing discrimination, however, he requires close supervision to prevent disastrous consequences. On the other hand, the insecure toddler may be so fearful of anything new that he will not undertake explorations that are potentially dangerous. He appears to be a child of unusual judgment unless it is recognized that he also does not explore that which is new but safe. Or he will explore everything but appear to learn nothing from painful explorations. Such a child may be confused with the really secure child; the diagnostic differentiation lies in the evidence for the presence or absence of an ability to discriminate between the dangerous and the safe and the resultant self-protective patterns of the secure child as against the unnecessary acceptance of painful situations by the insecure child who "lives dangerously."

Whenever the experience that provides the individual a sense of security is in part provided by his own efforts, the result is an increase in confidence in the self. This self-confidence originates from two broadly different situations. If, for example, the toddler succeeds through his own activity in attaining a toy he seeks, this act contributes to his sense of self-adequacy, and thus to security. On the other hand, he may not be able to achieve fulfillment of his wish for the toy. He charms his mother and indicates his need. She responds both to his pleasant mood and to his communication and gives the toy to him. He then feels self-confident, but not in terms of his first order of achievement, getting hold of the toy. A second order of achievement, however, has been effective. He develops confidence in the effectiveness of his personality even though his motor behavior is inadequate. Either experience constructively enhances his self-appreciation and self-love.

If the child, either by his own first order of behavior or by the second order of behavior through his involvement with others, is unable to attain his goal, his confidence in himself either fails to develop or is undermined. He does not like himself or trust himself anymore than he likes or trusts those adults around him who fail to meet his desires. The result is anxiety. He has a sense of helplessness accompanied by self-devaluation and the loss of self-love.

With the striving for security in the framework of the role of the self and the role of others, two new psychological structures—the ego ideal and the superego—begin to develop. They become a further source of security for the child.

The Ego Ideal
and The Superego

THE DEVELOPMENT OF AFFECTIVE NEEDS and responses parallels the development of a sense of self. The affective response referred to in Chapter 4 as primary narcissism comes to be expressed in patterns of behavior that assure the individual's physical and psychological survival and growth through his own iniative. And it is also manifested in an urge to be loved by the self and by others. From this urge develop the ego ideal and the superego. The ego ideal is based on an idealized conceptualization of the self that the individual can value and love because, if attained, it provides assurance of the gratification the individual seeks. It is an outgrowth of the earlier phase of primary narcissism and the cathexis of the self.

Achievement, particularly if it is acceptable to the parents and is rewarded by a positive response from them, is a pleasurable experience. Because this experience is self-achieved, the self is gratified and that configuration of the self is loved. In contrast, an act that cannot be achieved or, if achieved, results in parental disapproval, leads to an unpleasant experience; the image of the self as initiator of the act becomes one that is not satisfying and is therefore unloved. A lovable self-image leads to pride in the self, a narcissistically gratifying experience. An unlovable self-image leads to shame.

Repetitive experiences with positive and negative self-definitions lead to a formulation of behavior patterns that, if followed, will result in self-appreciation, self-love, and confidence that the self can provide gratification. They also provide a concept of those behavioral patterns that will lead to frustration of basic needs, displeasure, and lack of confidence in the self. From a series of such contrasting experiences evolves an ideal model for the self: the ego ideal. Once the broad definition of the ego ideal is established, the individual is no longer dependent on chance success or failure for positive results from his behavior; it is a yardstick for evaluating anticipated behavior. Compliance with the ego ideal then leads to confidence and pride in the self. Failure to live up to the ego ideal leads to shame, both in regard to actual behavior and to anticipated behavior.

It should be borne in mind that punishment involves more than physical punishment. The most painful punishment a child can receive is the real or imagined withdrawal of love. Loss of love and loss of all that love means to the child in terms of security and self-esteem is an experience that a child will avoid at tremendous cost to his own freedom. Early in psychological development the avoidance of punishment is a conscious act. The child learns from experience what behavior will result in punishment and what behavior will not. With the development of the superego, not only are the standards of the parent accepted by the child as his own standards (an aspect of the ego ideal) but the punitive response of the parent to unacceptable behavior is also incorporated into the individual's reaction to his own failure. The superego is an "internalized parent" that threatens punishment and that punishes for unacceptable behavior. Both the affect related to a threat to violate internalized standards and an act that violates those standards result in a sense of guilt. One of the forms of self-initiated punishment is the withdrawal of self-love, a punishment for violation of the ego ideal. Thus, the ego ideal becomes a part of the superego.

The meaning of guilt dynamically speaking is not clear. There is a component of anxiety in it which suggests that it is a particular form of anxiety related to the unconscious fear of punishment by the self. With guilt a fear of punishment from an outside source is often verbalized. This guilt probably has two components: It may be a projection of the internal punitive attitude on an external object in order to represent symbolically the amorphous, probably unconscious, self-punitive response; it may also be a response to an earlier anxiety. Parental punishment, feared in the past but now considered by the superego to be deserved punishment for a present act, is feared as punishment by substitute parental figures such as the law or a social group. Guilt also has many aspects suggesting that it *is* punishment more painful than other forms.

Guilt is relieved if the individual is punished by an outside source or by self-punishing acts that are physically or mentally painful. Doing penance, whether demanded by others or by the self, relieves guilt. At one time the origin of the superego was considered to be related to the resolution of the oedipal conflict. The oedipal conflict and its resolution have a marked effect on both the ego ideal and the superego; but observations of children indicate that the origin of both ego and superego precedes the oedipal period. The overt manifestations of both are easily recognized during the anal stage. The oedipal conflict only intensifies and broadens their functioning.

Value of the Ego Ideal and the Superego

The ego ideal and the superego, once they take shape, function for the most part unconsciously, although the behavior they cause can often consciously be explained by the feeling accompanying or following the forbidden behavior. The value of these two psychological structures is an economic one. They enable the individual to act spontaneously without having to evaluate each act or part of an act before it is carried out. They establish certain well-tried and safe pathways with appropriately placed signs warning against the dangers of following tracks that lead into dangerous areas. If these warning signs are not seen, an adventure down a track leading to dangerous consequences stimulates guilt or shame. In theory, a healthy superego and ego ideal are signs on the path that cannot be ignored; they warn against only seriously dangerous pathways. In actuality, signs are always missed and guilt and shame are experienced. There are too few or too many signs; the consequent guilt and shame are too severe and paralyze further exploration down a possibly nondangerous pathway, or they are too weak and allow the person to explore paths that lead to serious consequences.

In terms of psychological development the ego ideal probably predates the superego. It is possible, however, that severe punishment at a very early age can result in a premature superego structure with no adequate structuralization of an ego ideal. This phenomenon may explain a type of character structure in which the individual appears to have a guilty response to any spontaneous behavior, with little concept of who he would like to be other than someone who effectively avoids punishment. Children who are seriously inhibited in their behavior sometimes appear to fall into such a category. The following case illustrates this.

Jane, an obese eleven-year-old, seemed to have certain responses suggestive of a minimal internalized image of herself but a very rigid superego. Her obesity served many purposes. It brought punishment from both internal and external sources. Many of her waking hours were passed in self-depreciating thoughts about her unattractiveness, and her parents constantly nagged her about her obesity, pointing out that no one could think she was attractive. This picture of parental depreciation dated back to very early childhood. Even during her infancy, before obesity had become a problem, her parents demanded high standards of behavior; failure to live up to those standards brought an open withdrawal of affection.

In therapy, only after Jane became aware that her therapist was concerned only about her happiness and not about her obesity did a new aspect of her problem become revealed. She had no real image of herself except as an obese person who should be punished. She had no idea of how to behave until she asked her mother or father. She did not know what her ideal for herself should be. Only gradually could she form an ideal for herself in relation to her interpersonal relationships with her peers, her school accomplishments, or her goals for her future.

For a long period in therapy she attempted to structure an ego ideal for herself that, although colored by the sophistication resulting from the impact of life experiences dealt with through the functioning of a very superior intelligence, actually had the basic naivete of the child of four who wants to be a cowboy one day and a fireman the next. Prior to therapy, what little ego ideal Jane had was determined primarily by the need to avoid punishment—loss of parental love. Gratification of her primary narcissism came solely from assurance of survival; she experienced no gratification from achievement that should have provided pleasurable pride. In such a situation it appears that the ego ideal is limited to that self-image that will avoid punishment and thus is more a result of, rather than a means of, superego formation.

Superego Development

The preceding discussion implies that the superego is always the incorporated punitive parent. This notion is the usual explanation for the superego. There are certain instances, however, that suggest another component. Johnny's situation, for example, illustrates an instance in which the origin of the superego is difficult to trace. From the standpoint of metapsychology, unfortunately, his treatment was carried out by a boarding school placement so that intensive therapy was not possible. From Johnny's standpoint the treatment was effective, at least at the time. Later developments are not known.

Eleven-year-old Johnny was referred to a child therapist for study because of severe constriction of activities. An intelligent child, he did well academically in areas where memory was involved. According to the school, he had no creative ability. He was never known to do anything wrong; he conformed to all rules with a literalness that left no opening for criticism. His parents could not understand the constriction observed in their child. They were atypical in their own behavior, indulging, as did the sophisticated group of which they were a part, in mildly nonconforming behavior which had no unpleasant consequences. Johnny lived his infancy and childhood in an era in which psychologically sophisticated parents accepted the dictum that all neuroses are the result of curbing a small child's spontaneous behavior. Because they were loving parents, wishing Johnny to grow into a nonneurotic adult, they placed no restrictions on him; he had imposed the restrictions on himself.

Johnny's explanation for his behavior was simple. He said his parents never told him what was right and what was wrong. He was not old enough to know, but he would feel uncomfortable if he did things he felt were "bad." The inhibition of behavior dated back to early childhood, preceding the time when peer group responses might have been punitive. On the therapist's recommendation, Johnny was placed in a school where reasonable but definite limits were imposed and a violation would result in definite but reasonable punishment. His abandonment of his rigidity was dramatic. Within a year he became a normally relaxed twelve-year-old with many manifestations of creative ability. It can be questioned whether his original problem was a rigid superego or simply an inhibition resulting from an inability to anticipate what the unknown would provide. He had frightening ideas that suggested he feared punishment if he were bad, rather than just that the unknown might prove to be dangerous.

This case illustration, presenting a rigidity of superego that is not readily attributable to overly punitive parental behavior, would suggest that the superego sometimes originates within the child's psychic structure rather than in the patterns of parental behavior.

Failure of Integration and Adaptation

As indicated in Chapter 6, there appears to be an inherent drive in living matter to integrate and adapt in response to multiple needs. Failure to achieve a pattern of integration exposes a child to chaos; failure to achieve a pattern of adaptation of inherent urges to reality is equally dangerous.

Five-year-old Harry presented a picture in which this dangerous chaos existed. An acute psychotic episode had been precipitated by his mother's refusal to buy him a toy he wanted. He became angry at his mother, expressing a wish to kill her by hitting her in a violent manner. Immediately, however, he shifted to clinging to her, begging her not to leave him and to "save" him. By the time Harry was seen for a diagnostic interview, his mother had not been able to be out of his sight for twenty-four hours. During that period she had been constantly buffeted either by his hostile attack or by his pathetic clinging; each phase followed the other without the intervention of an external event that might explain the shift.

Harry gave the therapist a surprisingly coherent description of his problem. He loved his mother but he was angry at her and wanted to kill her. If he killed her, he would not have her. If he did not kill her he still kept wanting to. Also, he wanted the toy. His manner and his facial expression were those of a terrified animal. He could achieve no integration of contradictory impulses nor could he make any adaptation to reality. He was in an acute anxiety state as a result of contradictory impulses for which he had no answer.

The strength of primitive impulses is the source of a type of anxiety that can be allayed only if the primitive impulses are brought under some kind of control. The superego is one mechanism by which such control can be effected, and an unacceptable impulse can be curbed by the threat of punishment. Adaptation to the conflicting impulses can be achieved by inhibiting the expression of the undesirable impulse. Such a psychological mechanism then becomes the source of an internally rooted superego. Parental punitiveness in such a situation only defines what impulses should be repressed and what impulses should be permitted expression. As the parents' punitive attitudes become incorporated into the child's developing superego, they serve to allay the anxiety that would be created by unintegrated impulses. The dire consequence of acting on unintegrated, nonadaptive impulses, then, is not only punishment by the parents but also the internally originating punishment, namely, anxiety. Thus, the superego is the incorporated parent who punishes as well as that aspect of the self that experiences anxiety from primitive, unintegrated impulses.

Incorporation of Parental Standards

The psychological phenomenon of incorporation of the parent, with the parent's image becoming a part of the child's psychological configuration, is manifested in many aspects of psychological development but is perhaps most universally demonstrable in the development of the ego ideal and the superego. Parental standards of both approval and disapproval have a determinative effect on the development of the ego ideal. In the development of the superego, the punitive parent becomes internalized, thereby coloring the individual's feelings about his spontaneous behavior. It is relatively easy to state that parental attitudes become a part of the child's attitude; but it is not clear why or how this process occurs.

To attempt any explanations one has to look again at the infant's early behavior. As the infant becomes aware of observable phenomena, he attempts to integrate the isolated abilities he possesses. This attempt is suggested in the response of smiling. The neonate's muscular development probably is such that a muscular "smile" is possible, but it is actually a grimace, related more to discomfort than to pleasure. Other people, however, smile at the infant because of pleasure. This aura of pleasure may then result in imitative behavior, which eventually leads to an expression of affect.

Similarly, with the development of other skills, and particularly with the psychological ability to evaluate behavior and its effectiveness, the small child begins to imitate the behavior of others and to evaluate its effectiveness. Cause and effect relationships become cognitively clear. With this development, what was originally imitative becomes a means of affect-charged gratification or lack of gratification. At first, acting like the parent is not being like the parent but being like the parent that imposes standards of behavior. It is said that the child now "identifies" with the parent. Rather, he identifies with only one aspect of the parent, the standard-setting part. This achievement is not, as it is with the smile, a means of expressing affect. Imitation now leads to a more significant development. It is a means by which to assure positively meaningful responses through accepting the standards of the parents, in this sense being the same as, or identifying with, the parents.

Imitation of parental standards is only partially responsible for the development of the ego ideal. More important, a self-set that brings a negative response from the parent is a threat to the child's primary narcissism; he needs a positive response. He accepts the parental standards of behavior as a model which, if followed, will assure the sought-after positive response and he incorporates these standards into his embryonic ideal for himself, thus protecting himself from the threat inherent in parental disapproval. The threat of parental disapproval is important in the development of the child's ego ideal because of his need for the security the parent provides.

The small child also consciously imitates the punitive parent before the superego becomes structured. Having done something of which he disapproves or for which he fears the disapproval of others, he will reprimand or slap himself, often using the parental form of punishment. This early imitative stage evolves into an identification with the punitive parent; the child becomes the same as the punitive parent and responds to his own behavior as the punitive parent would be expected to respond. This identification with the punitive parent probably serves at first to avoid real punishment by blocking behavior through the curbing effect of anticipation of punishment. With the formation of the superego the identification with the parent finally results not only in the threat of self-imposed punishment but also in self-punishment if self-accepted rules are violated. This maturational step enables the child to assure himself that he can avoid pain by complying with his own ego ideal.

[14]

Object Relationships
and Ambivalence

SIMULTANEOUSLY WITH THE encompassing love of self characteriz-
ing the anal stage of development explored earlier, another affective
change is occurring—a more encompassing relationship with objects.
The child comes to love the object not only as a functional extension
of himself but as an object per se. Love of the object becomes more
abstract, less obviously a response to the function it serves. At this
point, the child has developed a capacity for what is termed "object
love" as distinguished from self-love.

At the risk of appearing too polemical, it would seem valid to argue
that all object love has its origin in primary narcissism and in the
functional role the object plays. Meaningful objects other than the
mother remain linked to the self by the same psychological cord.
Equally, a loved object is never completely severed from the self as
long as it remains meaningful. Even negatively meaningful objects
retain a link with the self. This concept is in contrast with the
Kleinian concept[1] in that it does not assume the cannibalistic incorporation of the good and bad mother. Rather it assumes that a
cathected object is a part of the person in terms of the perception of
the object and the emotional response to that perception. The early
unity of mother-object-child is thus retained in an abstract form.

The child now experiences objects as a source of gratification and
frustration of emotional needs. These needs have been broadened as
a result of the advance in the child's psychological maturational
development. The objects are loved not only because they serve for
physiological survival but also because they serve for psychological
survival. For man to survive as a total psychological and somatic
organism his survival needs, which are unique to the species, must be
met. Objects that can gratify those unique needs, as a result of the
more complex neurological system which enables the human being

1. Melanie Klein, *The Psychoanalysis of Children* (New York: Grove Press, 1960),
   p. 57.

not only to learn more but also to feel more, are objects that are the most meaningful to him. They are the objects he loves most if they gratify him and hates most if they fail to gratify him.

With increasing skill, a human being can gratify his basic physiological needs by his own acts. However, the objects to which the neurologically and emotionally mature individual relates are not those required to alleviate hunger and provide warmth; they are those that gratify the other needs of the human species, but which the individual cannot gratify himself because, by definition, they require another person. That the early origin of object relationships is not lost is evidenced in the symbolic use made of those needs and their gratification. For example, the expression "the warm love" shown by another is an example of the symbolic use made of an earlier actual somatic experience. Narcissistic cathexis and object cathexis are fused at this point.

With the development of a meaningful object relationship, a new conflict can be recognized. This conflict can be traced to the contradictory biological impulses of the very young infant, which are brought into some degree of harmony by the integrative-adaptive drive. For example, the neonate may be both hungry and tired; the urge for food and the need for sleep are in conflict. He sleeps and sucks at the same time in an effort to gratify both needs. The sucking is not satisfying, and he awakens to eat. The acute hunger allayed, he falls back to sleep in spite of inadequate nutritional consumption. Having relieved the need for sleep and with the hunger again increasing, he awakens to eat more. It is perhaps not too farfetched to call this a solution to "biological ambivalence." During the anal period of development and from that time on there is evidence of the inadequacy of the integrative-adaptive drive to resolve conflictual feelings. Ambivalence becomes discernible; the child loves and hates the same object.

Origins of Ambivalence

Ambivalence has been conceptualized by many as the result of the child's experiencing both the "good mother" who is giving and not frustrating and the "bad mother" who not only fails to give and frustrates but is held responsible for *everything* in the external world that is not giving and is frustrating. This concept of the early separation of the "good mother" from the "bad mother" is based in part on the assumption that the child does not relate to the mother as a whole but to a part of her. The infant's response to the breast is considered to be relatedness to a partial object, separate from the mother. With his growing ability to perceive the total object, the child comes to see that the good parts and the good mother and the bad parts and the bad mother are all one.

It is a clinical observation that, during the latter part of the second year of life, children will refer to the frustrating mother as a bad mother, the giving mother as a good mother. If this is indeed fractionating the mother so that she becomes two people, the mother also fractionates the child. The mother tells the obedient child that he is a good child, the refractory child that he is a bad child. It is not surprising that the child imitates the mother's manner of speech. It is possible that the child's concept of the good mother and the bad mother is an unconscious wish that he could have had both a good mother and a bad mother and so would have been able to love one and hate the other without having to deal with the conflict inevitable in ambivalent feelings toward the same love object.[2]

René A. Spitz has indicated that the neonate's first visual experience in relationship to the mother is the mother's face rather than the breast.[3] When the infant begins to perceive the child-care person's face, a mask worn by the adult will prevent a response. From this observation, it is assumed that the infant fractionates the mother, but one can question who does the fractionating. The face is the infant's guidepost for identifying the mother; it does not necessarily mean that the face is the total perception.

Before one is justified in stressing this early "partial object" concept, there needs to be more study of the bottle-fed baby, of the baby who is fed by a nurse but for whom the mother plays a role in other experiences, and of those infants who are cared for by one foster mother and are moved later to another foster mother. Within the limits of present knowledge it seems plausible to suggest that the infant does not "relate" to a fractionated object but rather that the object is experienced in a variety of ways. Later, as the child is able to identify the source of those experiences they are integrated into a concept of the mother. When the child is able to conceptualize the

2. A fantasy twin or an imaginary companion in many instances enables the child to fractionate himself in this way, with the imagined person being the bad part of the child. This self-fractionation is not demonstrable until the latter half of the second year or the third year of life and would appear to be a development made possible by the intellectual growth of the child.
3. René A. Spitz, "Object Relationship and Ambivalence," *The First Year of Life* (New York: International Universities Press, 1965), p. 81.

interrelatedness of his experiences, the mother is seen as a person who is, from the child's point of view, both lovable and hateful.

When the child begins to respond emotionally to the mother, ambivalence is inevitable. The mother who frustrates the child cannot be manipulated by his use of his own skills, and the frustration arouses the affective emotion of hostility. The small child's means for expressing hostility are limited, and his typical response is to attack physically. The child senses that this primitive impulse toward the parent is dangerous, for if he carried it out he might destroy a needed person who is also a loved person. Because this stage of development is one in which the need for the parent is great and the parent is frequently frustrating, it is the period in which ambivalence in the child's relationship to primary love objects is strongest. The child is sufficiently mature to identify both his positive and his negative feelings. The intensity of his ambivalent feelings decreases as he gradually understands more of the reasons for his frustrations.

There is another significant facet to the child's ambivalence. He assumes that his parents experience ambivalent feelings in the same fashion he does. In his fantasy, when they are crossed, the parents' impulse is also to destroy. This notion is confirmed by two of the child's ideas. Punishment, if it is in physical form, is an act of token destruction inflicted on the child by the parent. When isolation is used as punishment, the child sees it as an "as if" situation for the parent; to the child, the parents are looking on him "as if" he were nonexistent. If the parents scold, the child believes that the parent is angry and he assumes that the parent resembles himself; because he does not love when he is angry the parent's anger represents a withdrawal of love. It is an untenable position for the child, just as is the threat of physical destruction or isolation.[4]

Because of the child's inability to integrate his ambivalent feelings and his assumption of equally conflictual feelings on the part of the parent, he is anxious and in conflict. He is often quite manifestly disturbed during this period. At times the disturbance is shown in night terrors, the context of which (if the child is able to recall or happens to verbalize while the dream is still vivid) is frequently that of being lost or unable to find some prized toy or person.

---

4. This comment is not meant to suggest that a child should never be scolded or punished. Part of the child's essential learning is to realize that these dire consequences of scolding or punishment do not occur.

Fantasied Parental Omnipotence

There is another aspect to object love that becomes more readily demonstrable later in life. The more consciously separate the loved object is from the self, the more the love of self appears threatened. That "love is blind" is not quite true; love is blinkered, and only those characteristics that are in the line of vision are valued by the individual. The parent is seen as omnipotent and omniscient. This view is usually explained on the basis of the child's observations that, within the framework of the child's limited ability and the parental skills that control the child's life, the parent does possess these characteristics. Furthermore, in order to feel secure in an unknown environment, the child has to believe that the parents are all-powerful and all-knowing in order to give him protection. There also appears to be an additional factor: the small child holds to the concept of the parents' omnipotence even in areas in which it proves not to be true. The parent tries to fix a toy but fails. The child still believes the parent can fix the next toy. The parent says the child should not engage in a certain activity because he will get hurt if he does. The child does it and does not get hurt. The parent cannot prevent it from raining, night from coming, and many other natural phenomena a child would prefer to have not happen. The child typically does not get angry at the parents' failure to exercise omnipotence, but he blinds himself to the areas in which the parents fail him.

The cause of this blinkered reaction in the small child is not clear. It would seem that in addition to the actual relative omnipotence of the parent as compared to the small child, and the need the child has to believe the parent is omnipotent as a protection against the danger that the child is incapable of combatting, there may be a third factor. Before the love object is consciously and sharply differentiated from the self, the omnipotence of the parent is the omnipotence of the child. A remnant of this illusion is seen when the older child says, for prestige-striving reasons, "My father is smarter than your father." It may be that the illusion of parental omnipotence occurs at times to protect the child's self-esteem indirectly. The omnipotent parent enhances or repairs a blow to the child's narcissism, and thus an attempt is made to deny the failings of the parent.

Whatever the origin of the child's concept of the omnipotent loved person may be, as the child becomes consciously separate from the loved person, a conflict arises. The blinkers now enable the child to maintain the fantasy of the omnipotent parent, but the result is that instead of being enhanced the self by comparison, is depreciated. The belief in parental omnipotence must be retained because of the security it offers the child, who is relatively weak compared to the parent and also is unable to protect himself. This recognition leads to self-depreciation. Furthermore, as soon as the self and the loved objects are seen as separate, the libidinal investment in the loved person depletes the energy available for narcissism. "Lovers' quarrels" are part of the ambivalence of the small child as well as of the adult. The narcissistic blow that comes with the investment of love in another becomes intolerable and the child reacts with a fantasy of his own omnipotence to repair the narcissistic wound.

Self-Omnipotence

The self-omnipotent fantasy of the child has long been recognized. It has been explained in part by reality. The infant or young child is, in a sense, "monarch of all he surveys." If he cries, something happens. If he crawls behind a certain object, if he laughs, takes his first step, says his first word, a parent is there to respond. He takes it for granted that he is an important person. This concept, although based on reality, is fantasized as even greater than it is. To feel sure in the world and to feel omnipotent is to be safe; thus, the fantasy allays anxiety. Equally it repairs the narcissistic damage done by the idealization of a love object. It is the child's means of denying his relative inadequacy as compared to both the real parent and the idealized, loved parent. The megalomania seen in an adult patient suggests that he has regressed to that period in infancy in which he saw himself as omnipotent. Perhaps it is more a regression to a pattern of narcissistic recovery than to the fantasy of omnipotence. He has a strong desire to do for himself, sometimes in areas of competence and sometimes in areas not so wisely chosen. His object relationships and his need to emancipate himself from the crippling problems with which these relationships threaten him normally result in an increased surge to achieve narcissistic gratification.

15

Phallic
and Oedipal Stage

AT ABOUT THREE YEARS OF age anal eroticism loses its dominance, giving way to the external genitalia, the penis, and the clitoris. This shift signifies that the child has reached the phallic stage of development. There is no demonstrable biological explanation for this shift as there is for anal dominance, which appears to be related to neurological development. Because the penis is responsive to sensory stimulation from birth, the later dominance of the eroticization of this organ cannot be related solely to neurological development. It seems valid to assume that the clitoris is equally responsive to stimulation from birth.

Masturbation

Evidence for erotic gratification from stimulation of the genitalia at this age is more easily documented than for the eroticization of other areas during early maturational development. Masturbation becomes either a secret or an open pleasure.

During the early process of body exploration the child discovers the external genitalia by chance and enjoys the sensation resulting from the stimulation touching offers. With sufficient coordination of his movements he will, having discovered this pleasure, repeat it. There is a difference, however, between the early and the later masturbatory activity. The early activity has a transient, casual nature and other stimuli readily interrupt it. This suggests that although this early masturbation is pleasurable, it does not result in the intensity of response that comes later.

During the later maturational stage, masturbation becomes a common activity, a normal manifestation typical of this stage of development unless it is observed to be utilized as a substitute for other needs. Masturbatory activity may lead to tension of great intensity followed by relaxation, a cycle that has much in common with the later mature orgasm. The child's body moves rhythmically during masturbation, his face is flushed, and he appears unaware of his surroundings unless they forcefully impinge on him.

It is interesting to observe the shame or guilt that children often show when they become aware that someone has observed this activity. In the past it was assumed that this response was because of parental prohibition against masturbation. But there is now a generation of parents who have, at least intellectually, accepted the idea that masturbation is not injurious and that its appearance is evidence of maturation in the child. The child, however, frequently continues to respond with shame or guilt when discovered, as if his behavior were forbidden.

There are several possible explanations for this response. Earlier masturbation is frequently interrupted by the parents, who reveal their impatience. The parental impatience is only indirectly related to the masturbation. The time the exploring infant is most apt to discover his external genitalia and the pleasure resulting from touching them is when he is being diapered. The parent, wishing to complete the diaper change, removes the infant's hands and becomes impatient if he resists. Probably in some cases, the child retains a memory of this event and anticipates parental disapproval. This explanation would seem to have some validity in those cases in which the child is never observed in masturbatory activity after this early exploration.

During the later age period there are two types of masturbation. One is an intense, orgastic-like response; the other is similar to the earlier pattern. In the latter type the child rubs his genitalia gently, does not become tense, may show no response of guilt or shame. The same child, however, when aroused to a point of tension while masturbating, may manifest guilt or shame. This latter picture can perhaps still be related to parental response. The many parents who intellectually accept the normalcy of masturbation find it difficult to control their own feelings about it. The intensity of the child's response calls forth the threat of a parallel excitation in the parent. The parent is disturbed by his own response and becomes tense, not on the basis of sexual excitation but because of his own unconscious prohibition against such gratification for himself. The child may then sense the parents' nonverbal disapproval of the behavior. How much the parental response is an inherent prohibition of masturbation and how much it is a relic of the parents' own childhood, only the passage of time will make clear. The teachings of puritanical forefathers may persist under the intellectual surface for many generations!

There is considerable clinical evidence that at least the orgastic type of masturbation is accompanied by fantasies that the child sees as unacceptable. These fantasies are revealed in the therapy of children of this age and later as well as in the recall of adult patients in analysis. The fantasies reported reveal the psychological significance of this maturational phase, suggesting that the guilt and shame observed in the child may be related to the fantasies or the intensity of the erotic response rather than to the masturbatory activities per se. This latter explanation has bearing upon the typical conflicts of this period, paralleling as it does other psychologically significant developments.

The Oedipal Stage of Development

With at least a partial resolution of the psychological conflicts of the earlier periods, three major psychological growth patterns reach a level of maturity and integration at about this age that, interdigitating with phallic eroticization, result in the total constellation referred to as the oedipal stage of development. These three patterns are: (1) the fusion of the instinctual drives, particularly the alloplastic drive and the libidinal drive—the latter the response to the need to be loved or to be cared for by a loving person; (2) the evolvement of object love from primary narcissism; and (3) the increased functioning of the intellectual components of the psyche—imagery, fantasy, and memory in particular. Individual children evidence different rates of maturation in each of these areas of development. Mild discrepancies in individual development are probably insignificant. If, however, a serious discrepancy occurs in one area of development the ultimate personality will be seriously crippled. The effect of that crippling often becomes discernible when, either at the time of the oedipal period or by later reconstruction of this period, the psychological difficulties are found to be related to ineffectual or unhealthy attempts at resolution of the oedipal conflicts.

As a child begins to love another person his primary love is for the person who has been most significant to him, usually his mother. Although she may be the chief recipient of this love, under ordinary circumstances she is not the only one to whom he responds in this fashion. During his life other people have also become the source of pleasure to him. Grandparents, siblings, nurses, maids, and neighbors, among others, have been meaningful to the child and now are also recipients of his love.

In certain cultures and in certain families in any culture the father is a feared rather than a loved figure. The typical picture in Western society is one in which the father, although at times a powerful and punishing figure, is also a person who warrants being loved. Prior to the oedipal period of development the father has shared in the care of the child, has played with him, has brought him toys, has taken him out for pleasant excursions, and has protected him. The father has been a source of essential security so that the child has not been solely dependent on the mother. Thus, the father generally is loved with an intensity second only to the response to the mother.

At the phallic-oedipal level there is a modification in the type of love response according to the sex of the child and the sex of the parent. The child typically responds with more intense love toward the parent of the opposite sex and withdraws some of his early affection from the parent of the same sex. This shift justifies the assumption of the sexual nature of the response. It should be borne in mind, however, that this is infantile sexuality; that it is the anlage of mature sexuality would appear noncontroversial.

Why this shift occurs is difficult to explain on any but teleological grounds. As a result of the differentiation, the foundation is laid for ultimate heterosexuality. There is a partial explanation, other than teleological, for this sexual differentiation in Western culture. Many months before the child reaches this maturational level he is encouraged to see himself in accordance with his own sex. Most often the little boy is treated as a boy, the little girl is treated as a girl. The child is encouraged to follow the behavior of the parent of the same sex. Toys are selected with that in mind. There is clinical evidence that if a little girl is treated as if she were a little boy and encouraged to act like a boy, she has a great deal of difficulty in accepting the fact that she is a girl. Regardless of the inherent factors that determine this maturational step, the environment of the child facilitates, retards or distorts the form it takes.

Another aspect of significance is undoubtedly the child's ability to recognize anatomical differences between the sexes. It is difficult to believe that as many children as claim not to know the anatomical differences have never made the observation. The recognition of sexual differences and the child's own self-identity as a boy or girl do not, however, fully explain the shift in love objects and the change in the nature of the affection.

Another possible contributing factor is that adults have a differing emotional reaction to a child, depending on the child's sex and the adult's general response to that sex. This adult response probably would reinforce any inherently determined difference in the child's response. But no one explanation for the shift in object love that occurs at this age period is entirely satisfactory. Parental response to the shift in love objects is determined by the characteristics of the relationship of both parents to the child as well as by the cultural patterns to which the child is exposed.

Up to this age level the psychological picture of maturation has been assumed to be the same irrespective of the sex of the child. Now, however, the child faces conflicts, the nature of which is determined by the child's sex.

The Boy During the Oedipal Stage

The little boy's first love object is typically his mother. It is she who meets his needs during neonatal life and during the oral stage of development. It is primarily in her that his sense of security is rooted. With the capacity for object cathexis, his positive response to her function in terms of his needs develops into love for her, no longer solely in terms of her care but now also on a less functional basis. He is still dependent on her, but superimposed on this dependency is his response of affection not directly related to her nurturing role. His libidinal drive is chiefly directed toward his mother, a love object of the opposite sex.

His maturational level and his capacity to love bring him into direct conflict with his father. In the framework of this new aspect of his libidinal response the father becomes his rival. The little boy envies his father's relationship with his mother and wishes to displace him. In a sense he wishes to return to a unity with his mother, to a unity that excludes others who apparently wish to have a similar relationship with her; he wishes to be the most important love object to her as she is to him. This wish to compete successfully with others brings him face-to-face with the problems his father presents and results in three broad areas of conflict.

First, there is a realistic difficulty in this rivalry situation. The father is much larger and much stronger. He is a rival with whom it is difficult to compete. In an attempt to win this uneven struggle, the child often attempts to attack the father verbally. Often in fantasy he imagines the father disposed of by death or permanent exclusion from the home. He may express a wish for the father to die. He may also compete with the father more indirectly by promising his mother pleasures his father does not provide: when he grows up he will build her a big house, give her a fine fur coat, and beat up any person who is not nice to her. He hopes she will realize that his virtues are clearly superior to those of his father.

The second area of conflict for the male child is reinforced by this attempt to woo the mother from the father. The little boy assumes that, in view of his mother's interest in him, his father may be jealous, just as he is. Because his father has the strength to avenge himself in a fashion the child would want to utilize were he able to do so, he fears his father will destroy him. His anticipation of his father's jealousy is not without some realistic foundation. As the little boy becomes less dependent on his mother and as he becomes more adept in handling his ambivalent feelings toward her, her response to him is modified. It is now discernibly different from her response to her daughter. She values him as a male child, not just as a child; in a diluted form she responds to him as she responds spontaneously to men. Unless her response reaches pathological proportions, this component of her affection for her son contributes to his healthy development in the long run. It provides the groundwork for his final heterosexual adjustment, in which there is basic confidence that his own masculinity is valued by a loved and loving woman.

The third area of conflict for the male child develops in any family in which the father has been a positive meaningful object to the child. The little boy basically values the father's love because it is rewarding; he does not wish to be deprived of it. He also loves his father. If he is competitive with his father, his father may withdraw his love, an unbearable consequence. His wish for his father's destruction is unacceptable because, if it should become a reality, he would not only lose a person who loves him but also one whom he loves. Even if he can master his anxiety concerning the consequences of his wish to replace his father without abandoning that goal, he is still not free of difficulties. His mother would not accept him as a replacement. He is a son whom she loves, but not potentially a person who is more gratifying as a husband than her husband is. The little boy is faced with the reality that he cannot replace the father because the mother would not accept him in that role. She wants her male child to be a son; her husband is in a category for which the child cannot qualify. This is a narcissistic blow to the boy and he experiences shame.

Presented in this theoretical and schematized form, the male child's conflict is sharply delineated. He wishes to replace his father; however, he fears to enter an open battle with a person obviously much more powerful than he. He fears the jealousy of the father with the implication of retaliative behavior. He does not wish to lose this loved person. Finally, he faces the reality aspect of his mother's response to him as a person.

During the acute stage of the oedipal conflict, and before the male child finds a consistently tenable answer, he vacillates between various potential solutions. At times he enters into direct rivalry with his father and openly woos the mother with promises. This strategy fails when the father returns in the evening, greeted by the mother with enthusiasm. Sometimes he will become openly rivalrous and express dissatisfaction when his parents appear to be congenial; he will make an effort to separate them. When, however, he and his father can share an adventure from which the mother is excluded, they often have a very enjoyable time, and one that the child will treasure.

Many parents report that weekends are the most difficult times in the family's life. The father is certain that the mother completely indulges the child in his absence and decides that when he is at home he will correct these bad child-rearing practices. He becomes more strict, thus confirming the little boy's belief that the father is a dangerous and jealous rival.

In the meantime, the mother is aware that the crises that occur in the evening and during the weekend do not occur with such frequency or vehemence during the time she is alone with her son. The variable, then, is the father. The symptoms have a rough correlation with the father's presence. She therefore decides that the father is too strict or in some way is creating a disturbance for the little boy. Her concept of corrective measures are diametrically opposed to those of the father. Meanwhile, the mother's attitude produces further tension in her son because it implies that he may be more important than his father and that she will be his ally against the father. Yet he must still recognize that his mother will not accept him as a replacement for the father.

When the little boy senses that the mother is condemning the father's child-rearing practices and thus sees her as his ally, he may show surprising anger toward her. The origin of this anger is sometimes more easily traced in the retrospection of adults than during the therapy of small children but it is at times discernible in the latter study. This anger has two components. First, by her behavior the mother seemed to promise him the reward of fulfilling his desire to replace the father. But she fails to accept him as a replacement and he is frustrated. Second, her behavior has exposed him to another danger. Her disagreement with his father reveals an implied preference for her son, thus inviting the father's jealousy of the boy. She has abandoned her protective role, leaving him in a very dangerous situation.

A possible solution to this impasse lies in his establishing a positive relationship with his father. The boy can turn his intensified libidinal investment toward his father rather than toward his mother. If he renounces his tie to his mother his reward will be a feeling of greater safety with his father. If his father is loved as well as feared, this is an even more gratifying solution; the renunciation of the mother is a sacrifice in the service of love for the father. However, if the child is to accept this treaty with either the feared or the loved and feared father he expects to be rewarded by replacing his mother in his father's affection. But his father does not give him this reward because his father is not willing to replace the mother with the boy in his affections. The father's response to the mother is that of a husband to wife, to his son that of father to son. This shift of conflict is often referred to as the negative oedipal phase.

As unsatisfactory as this solution is, it has certain serviceable aspects. The little boy finally represses his wish to replace the father by repressing the infantile sexual implications of his love for his mother. He can then love his mother without being a rival to his father. He accepts the nonsexual aspects of his father's pattern of response to her, becoming equally thoughtful and protective. He attempts in other ways to be like his father, and his conceptualization of himself as a potential man takes definitive form. His father becomes the model for his ego ideal, and his superego also becomes more crystallized. It is now not formulated on the basis of parental standards; it is more definitely defined by the standards the father represents.

The ego ideal and the superego, as they attain crystallization with the resolution of the oedipal conflict, are not, however, defined solely by acceptance of the father's standards. The mother still represents a person by whom it is important to be loved. In her criticism and praise of both her husband and her son she indicates the kind of man to whom she would most freely give her love. Therefore, in those areas in which the father does not live up to the mother's dream the boy still tries to better him. Now, however, it is more in terms of the person he wishes to become rather than with the idea of wooing the mother in competition with the father.

With the renunciation of the infantile sexual wishes toward the mother and with identification with the father and the mother's fantasy ideal of a man, the final stones of the foundation of the child's ego ideal and superego are cemented into a basic personality structure. The superstructure that is built during the next developmental period, latency, may present surprising configurations, but it will be limited by the form the basic structure takes. During adolescence the foundation will be threatened, but the adhesiveness that binds the parts of the foundation for the ego ideal and superego is very tenacious and a modification of the superstructure rarely results in a structure completely free of the limits imposed by the basic structure. The identification with the father that is so important during the resolution of the oedipal conflict is sequentially probably not the first identification. As the infant comes to differentiate the self from the object, he identifies with an object that is loved. Thus, a small child's first identification, regardless of his or her sex, is with the child-caring person, essentially the mother. The tender care the mother gives to the child is probably one source of tenderness in later life. Thus, during the oedipal period the little boy does not have to shift his previous love object; his mother remains the major libidinally cathected object. However, in order to resolve the oedipal conflicts healthily, he does have to shift his identification from the mother to the father. This shift is easiest if the father is also a tender person. But, because masculine tenderness in our culture is often expressed differently from feminine tenderness, this switch in identification is often made only after a period of confusion.

The preceding description of the oedipal phase of development for the male child is presented in a skeletal outline of relatively normal conflicts and resolution of those conflicts during that period of maturation. In fact, the problems that are faced during this age span are typically much more complex. Although it is impossible here to go into a detailed description of even the major vicissitudes of this period, certain familiar constellations should at least be mentioned. If the father is not a loved person, only a feared person, the little boy may still identify with the father in order to protect himself from hostile attacks but his identification is then with the father's hostile strength and an unpleasant, hostile personality can evolve in the child. Alternatively, instead of identifying with the hostile parent the boy may passively submit to the father, renouncing his drive to compete with his father and reconciling himself to a self-image of inadequacy in comparison, becoming anxious whenever that self-image is threatened. The classical example of this reaction in adult life is the man who can work hard for success but, when he achieves it, becomes either paralyzed by anxiety or reacts in a way to destroy his success. He cannot tolerate being as or more effective than his father or his father as represented by a superior.

On the other hand, the father may be rejected as an object for identification while the mother continues to be the object with whom to identify. This can be related to two different situations. The father's standards may be culturally quite acceptable, but the mother does not consider them so. The child may not be able to reject the mother's standards because he feels that she would probably withdraw her love if he did so. In contrast, the mother's standards of behavior may be more acceptable to the culture of which the child is a part than those of the father. Identification of the child with the unacceptable standards of the father would lead to painful consequences. Acceptance of the mother's standards, if a masculine figure with similar standards is not available, may be a wiser identification, although identification with the mother can lead to a truly feminine identification and a renouncement of all masculinity. Identification with another person with the mother's standards does not necessarily resolve the problem.

As another possibility, the mother may be the more feared person because she is so often the principal disciplinarian. This fear may be valid. The little boy may then assume that safety lies only in submission to the mother, particularly if the father implies by his behavior that submission is the only solution to the family situation. In such a situation, the child accepts the mother's restrictive attitudes as a result not only of his fear of defying them, but also in many instances as a result of his identification with the father and the father's response to the mother.

Perhaps the most difficult situation a male child can face is one in which the parents respond in a fashion that makes the child's fantasy of a triangular situation a reality. A woman, either because of an unfortunate marriage or because of her own emotional immaturity, may in reality prefer her son to her husband and may attempt to have her child subtly meet those needs that a husband would meet for a more mature woman. She overstimulates the child, implying that he can replace the husband but, ultimately, denies the possibility. The little boy grows into a man who believes that the promise may finally become an actuality. He may then become an overly devoted adult son or a man who repeatedly conquers a woman only to abandon her because the woman he really wishes to conquer is his mother and no woman serves as an adequate substitute.

Similarly, the immature father seeking a kind of gratification from his wife that is more characteristic of that sought from a mother figure may in reality resent the mother's emotional investment in the son. The rivalry situation then becomes a reality. As the child grows older he may manifest one of many residual effects. He may deny the rivalry by wooing the jealous father or a symbolic representation of the father, denying his interest in the opposite sex. He may reject all women for fear his acceptance of one woman will reactivate the father's jealousy or the jealousy of other men. On the other hand, he may be interested only in women in whom other men are interested, losing interest once the other men withdraw from the field of competition. These are only a few of the many distortions that can result from this kind of family constellation.

The Girl During the Oedipal Stage

The female child deals with certain problems similar to those faced by the boy in the oedipal period, but there are differences. Like the boy, she first identifies with the mother. However, where the boy must renounce, or at least modify, this early identification in order to establish his masculinity, the little girl, with maturation, only expands her patterns of identification with the mother to encompass not only the role of tender caring but also that of feminine sexuality.

On the other hand, the oedipal level of maturation presents the little girl with a more anxiety-arousing situation than it does the little boy. Her powerful rival is the person who has also been the source of her security. Thus, hostility toward the mother and competition with her may result in a retaliatory response that can be devastating, the withdrawal of that which has made the world seem safe to her. The little boy may conceive of his father's attempting to destroy him; the little girl may conceive that the mother not only would attempt to retaliate destructively but also would expose her to the unknown dangers inherent in the world were she not provided some maternal sheltering. For this reason the little girl often has a more difficult time than the little boy in resolving the conflicts of the oedipal period, and women more often than men show serious scars as a result of the unsuccessful resolution of these conflicts.

A little girl's attempts at a solution and her ultimate resolution of these conflicts, under optimum conditions, have the same components as do those of the boy. She identifies with the parent of the same sex, represses the infantile sexual component of a relationship with her father, and solidifies her ego ideal and superego by incorporating more completely the standards of the mother. She modifies the part she accepts from her mother on the basis of her conceptualization of the kind of woman that approximates her father's image of the feminine ideal.

This schematic formulation describes the oedipal period as defined in theory, but in reality it is rarely so clear. The parents' personalities and their response to the child influence the final outcome of the oedipal conflict for the boy or the girl. Except by very detailed study it is often difficult to discern the interrelationships in the family. Parental responses to the child may be rooted in their own deeply unconscious needs, and the expression of these needs may be disguised by cultural patterns.

Significance of Parental Behavior

The underlying meaning of parental behavior rather than the overt behavior itself and the effect on the child can be illustrated by the practice of parents exposing themselves to their children in the nude. The original rationale for this behavior, which was very popular in the early 1920s, was that children's conflict over sexuality was in part due to curiosity that could be satisfied only by forbidden exploration. It was assumed that if parents showed no shame about their own bodies the child could satisfy his own curiosity without guilt and feel no shame about his own body. Clinical material gathered later indicates that such experiences were very disturbing for many children. The little boy, in observing that his father's penis was much larger than his own, felt humiliated and even more inadequate. He was also frightened by observing that his mother did not have a penis, a seeming confirmation of the validity of his castration anxiety. Furthermore, he was sexually stimulated by his mother's exhibition-ism, a stimulation that he could not yet handle adequately. The little girl was frightened by the sight of her father's penis and also sexually excited by his exhibitionism. Her mother's genitalia, hidden by pubic hair, mystified her. Thus, because of the clinical evidence that observing parents in the nude is disturbing to the children, parents were soon advised to resume the former patterns of modesty. The child should learn about anatomical differences from observing nude children of both sexes of his own age or younger.

In reality, modesty can be just as stimulating as exhibitionism. In addition, coy secretiveness intensifies the child's curiosity. Probably the most significant factor is the parent's unconscious use of modesty or exhibitionism as an expression of his or her own feelings. The parental exhibitionism of the 1920s would not have been so disastrous to certain children had the parents been free of their own problems.

This example has been used to point out that it is not *what* parents do but the *way* they do it that is of significance in the child's oedipal phase of development. What parents do is determined by their conscious philosophy of child rearing; how they do it is determined primarily by their own psychological format, colored chiefly by unconscious conflicts and inadequate solutions to their own earlier conflicts.

Because the parents' responses and goals during this phase of child rearing can be so disguised by the unconscious, parental guidance for those genuinely seeking advice is often only relatively effective and may add to further confusion for the child.

Castration Fears and Penis Envy

During the phallic-oedipal stage the external genitalia have a great deal of meaning to the child and become a focal point for fears and anxieties. The common root of these anxieties is the boy's fear of castration and the girl's concern about the absence of a penis. Although the concept that all little boys fear castration at this developmental stage has been challenged, the material from analytic child therapy and the dreams and associations of adults suggests that some degree of such anxiety is almost universally experienced. Castration anxiety is demonstrable; the castrating figure may be either the father, the mother, or both.

Harry is an example. He had two constant imaginary companions, a dog and a cat, who were in almost constant battle. One animal threatened to attack Harry; the other protected him. During the fantasized battle, Harry would become tense with fear. The protecting animal, however, always won the battle; whether it would win the war was never clear to Harry. The striking aspect of this fantasy, however, was that sometimes the dog was the attacker and sometimes the cat was. It became clear in therapy that the dog represented Harry's father, the cat, his mother. Long before Harry understood that the attack represented a threat to his penis, during the fantasy he would place his hand protectively over his genitalia. It became clear in therapy that he feared castration by both parents, but never at the same time. There was a superficial reason for this shift in the feared person. His parents quarreled frequently, claiming that the quarrels were about him. At times his father said that Harry was an impossible boy; he should be a girl. To this the mother responded that the father was to blame because he did not want to allow Harry to be a boy. The "dog" was threatening Harry and the "cat" was protecting him. At other times his mother would say that Harry was impossible; she did not like boys anyway and she wished he were a girl. His father then defended him. The dog now protected Harry from the cat's attack. No wonder Harry was chiefly preoccupied with his castration anxiety.

Is castration anxiety always rooted in the fear of the actual loss of the penis because it is of such value to the little boy? Or is it sometimes anxiety related to the penis as a symbol of masculinity and sexual identity? If it is the latter, the loss of the penis means the loss of that identity. If the latter is a component of castration anxiety, it may explain why frequently maturation does not abolish this fear. In the analysis of adult males who manifest neurotic symptoms related to castration, anxiety often persists even though the man recognizes that an actual castration threat does not exist. What he really fears is the destruction of his masculine identity.

Characteristically, the little girl in the oedipal stage envies the boy for possessing a penis, although in some instances, envy predates this stage. When early envy is experienced it probably becomes enhanced at the oedipal period, its significance largely dependent on the nature of the multiple internal and external psychological stimuli which the child must master at this time.

Apart from the deeper psychological reasons for penis envy there are many realistic factors that foster it. Many little girls verbalize and women recall envy of the little boy's urinary freedom and the equipment he has for urinary exhibitionism. Even if the little girl urinates in front of others there is little or no exhibitionistic gratification in it. She may often try to urinate standing up in order to acquire techniques that will enable her to be exhibitionistic. In some cases it is not the penis per se that she wants; it is the exhibitionism.

Although there are some theoretical arguments against universal penis envy, in reality many little girls are consciously envious and wish to have a penis. A little girl may fantasize that her clitoris will grow and become a penis. Or she may fantasize that she had one and lost it either because of a destructive act of another or because of her own destructiveness. The formation of the external genitalia may confirm her concept; the labia suggests a deep scar. She may also fantasize that she has a penis but it is hidden inside of her to remain always her secret.

Unless a little girl attains some satisfactory solution to her envy of the little boy, her adjustment to an adult role will be difficult. The most effective solution results from identification with a mother who has achieved a level of mature identification in her feminine role, has lost her envy, and feels a nonenvious respect for the masculine role. One can assume that such a maturational pattern in women and a complementary maturational pattern in men have not been achieved by any large numbers of people, so long as "the battle of the sexes" and the high frequency of neurotic sexual adjustment still persist.

Crystallization of the Ego Ideal and the Superego

The superego and the ego ideal become more firmly crystallized with the resolution of the oedipal conflict. By this time also the ego ideal and superego are sufficiently enmeshed so that a sharp demarcation between the two is not possible. Before the crystallization of the ego ideal and the superego is complete there is often a relative change in their form. Prior to the oedipal age the development of the ego ideal and superego was influenced by the parents as a unit or individually, but not in accordance with their sexual differences. Because the mother is in more contact with the child than the father, she probably contributes the dominant part in the formulation of each. The oedipal period establishes the parents as definers of good and bad, not as a unit but as individuals representing more clearly delineated patterns.

As a result of the healthy resolution of the oedipal conflict, the superego is more directly influenced by the parent of the same sex. The ego ideal is also chiefly influenced by the parent of the same sex, but it is colored by the indications the parent of the opposite sex gives of the type of person that is considered desirable. When circumstances make this modification of the ego ideal and superego difficult, identification with the person of the same sex also becomes difficult or impossible.

16

Anxiety

ANY DISCUSSION OF ANXIETY INVOLVES the need for semantic clarification. In some writings anxiety and fear are used interchangeably. In the context of this material, however, they are differentiated, permitting a clearer vocabulary for tracing the development of neurotic anxiety through the fears and anxieties of childhood. The term is used in this discussion to indicate the response of an individual to a realistic present danger. The term "anxiety" is used to indicate the response to an anticipated danger, whether the anxiety is neurotically determined or is realistically based on past experiences.

In discussing both anxiety and fear it should be borne in mind that anyone's response to a situation is dependent in part on his ability to comprehend it. What one person fears may be responded to by another with rational or neurotic anxiety. Elements of all three responses are likely to be found in any individual's response to most situations that produce fear or anxiety. Clinically it is that response which is dominant that is important in evaluating its significance.

These differentiations are possible in the description of child development because of the gradual and sequential evolvement of the child's psychic structure. Neurotic anxiety in childhood typically has developed from a fear of an immediate situation, followed by justified anticipatory anxiety.

This developmental picture can perhaps be demonstrated by a hypothetical situation. A small child may be afraid when he is first confronted by a barking dog as large or larger than himself. Nothing in his experience has assured him that the animal is not dangerous or has taught him that it is dangerous. His affective response is one of fear as a result of his self-preservative response that is stimulated by the threat the dog represents. If the dog knocks him down, his fear is justified and the animal's next appearance will arouse the same affect. Later, the anticipation of seeing a dog will stimulate an affective response. When told that there is a dog in the house where

155

he is to visit, he may respond with anxiety. His response is not to an object but to an abstraction that will become reality in the future. Neither the original fear nor the later anxiety is irrational. Within the scope of his ability to evaluate, he has learned that dogs are dangerous; their presence arouses fear in him, and the anticipation of seeing them creates anxiety. Within the semantic framework used here, a child cannot experience anxiety until he has reached the developmental level at which cognitive memory is possible.

If this child has a series of experiences with large dogs who prove to be friendly and desirable playmates, his anticipatory anxiety and his fear when confronted with a dog will ordinarily disappear. If, however, his first experience with the dog or a subsequent fear-arousing experience occurred at a time when he was attempting to master some conflict, the dog may become a symbol of that conflict. Perhaps this encounter occurred at a time when he was attempting to establish his individuality through "negativism" and he was confronted by a parental response that was punitive. His fear of the punitive parent may become fused with his fear of the dog because the two fears were experienced at the same time. As the child becomes aware of ways to avoid punishment and also aware that even the punitive side of parents is not such a threat to survival or the establishment of individuality, the intensity of his fear of the parent ordinarily decreases. In some instances, however, the fear must be repressed or denied if the child is to feel free to grow. Instead of completely repressing or denying the fear, the child can partially discharge it through fear of the dog, and the dog becomes the symbol of the dangerous parent. The child then develops an irrational fear of dogs; diagnostically he has a dog phobia.

Differentiating between Fear and Anxiety

In some respects the differentiation between fear, anxiety and neurotic anxiety can be diagnosed more readily in children than in adults. In a child fear and nonneurotic anxiety are less contaminated by neurotic components. From another viewpoint, they are more difficult to differentiate in children because neurotic anxiety in a child is often not as fixed and as difficult to reverse as it is in the adult. There are many instances to illustrate this in the commonly found anxiety about animals. Many small children show an anxious response to all large animals, or to a certain species. The parents trace the response to some unpleasant experience. The child, for example, was frightened in the past by a large dog and from that time on has feared all dogs. To change this behavior, the parents buy a dog and, after a few timid advances to the animal, the child no longer fears the dog but in actuality becomes very attached to it. Later other dogs also will be nonfrightening. Such a history suggests that the original anxiety was the result of a frightening experience, and a pleasurable experience with a pet erased the effect of the earlier one. If one judges this outcome by the tenaciousness of phobic states in adults it would appear justified to assume this is not a neurotic response on the part of the child. His ready modification of his behavior when provided with reassuring experiences would indicate that his earlier anxiety had, within his ability to evaluate a situation, justification. Sometimes the further history of the child's responses does not confirm this benign diagnosis. Although his fear of dogs may have disappeared, he may have developed anxiety responses to a series of stimuli, one given up only to be replaced by another. The parents may indicate that the child has always been a fearful child who becomes anxious in any new situation until he gains familiarity with it. This reaction suggests an underlying neurotic anxiety for which the symbolic representation of the stimulus changes over time but in which the core of the difficulty remains unmodified.

On the other hand, clear neurotic anxiety in a child may clinically disappear with surprising ease. Probably only if extensive therapy is undertaken in adulthood will it become clear whether the basic source of anxiety was really alleviated. The consolation to the child therapist in such cases is that at least the core problem no longer prevents clinical manifestations of healthy, psychological development.

Fear

Fear, in its most uncontaminated form, is an emotional response with which all individuals have had some experience; it is an affective response to an external threat of danger to the self. But this affective response does not always accompany danger; it is a reaction to danger only when there is not complete confidence that the danger can be mastered. If the danger can be mastered, the self is not threatened and fear does not result. For example, it is theoretically dangerous to dive from a high diving board. A threat of being pushed off the board would arouse fear in a person who was unable to swim. An experienced diver, on the other hand, would without fear do a complicated dive before safely entering the water. The danger to both individuals is the same. The competence or incompetence of the individual to handle the dangerous implications determines whether the individual experiences fear. (The experienced diver may experience anxiety, but such anxiety typically has neurotic components.

Fear is aroused particularly in childhood when the child faces a situation that, within his ability to evaluate, is a dangerous one; he feels unable to deal with it himself, and no reliable source of protection is available to him in his immediate environment. If the situation proves to be easy to handle, a recurrent one of similar nature is typically met with confidence and no fear is experienced. If it is not adequately handled and anticipation of its recurrence creates anxiety, its actual recurrence results in fear. Often the child's initial or final success in handling the situation is the result of another person either assisting him in exploring its implications in order to discover that with further knowledge the danger conceived does not exist, or assisting him to handle the danger so that he need not fear it.

Returning to the small child's fear when first confronted with a large dog, one can delineate two possibilities. First, by evidencing no fear of the dog and by gradually bringing dog and child together, the adult may enable the child to reevaluate the giant and recognize its harmlessness. Or second, the adult may demonstrate a proper approach to the dog; he may talk quietly to it, approach it slowly, and finally gently pet it, encouraging the child to imitate his behavior. The child then does not reevaluate dogs, seeing them subsequently as always harmless, but rather learns how to approach a potential danger in a way that masters the danger.

Parents and other adults often are so eager to protect a child from fear that they fail to encourage healthy fear. Fear of a reality situation that an individual does not have the tools to handle is a valuable affect in the service of preservation of life. For example, it is valid for a child to be taught to fear crossing a street until he has the judgment to handle the dangers involved in doing so. There are many potential dangers in daily life that a child should fear until his stage of development enables him to handle them adequately.

Biological Basis for Anxiety

During maturation from birth to adulthood there are many dangers that, if unmasterable or unmastered, lead to anxiety. If they come to serve as symbolic representations of a facet of neurotic conflict, they are stimulants for neurotic anxiety. These dangers occur because of the basic needs of the individual and because of aspects of the maturational pattern. They become the source of neurotic anxiety as a result of the failure to resolve normal maturational conflicts. With the development of the psychic structure the response to danger becomes psychosomatic. The perception of danger stimulates the flow of adrenalin and the somatic signs of anxiety become manifest. The rapid respiratory and cardiac rates and the muscular alertness then become a physiological response initiated by the increased activity of the adrenal glands under stress. Under the stress of fear or anxiety the somatic aspects are readily discernible. Individuals with a minimum of neurotic anxiety will also manifest anxiety when physical conditions lead to rapid heart beat or respiratory acceleration. Patients with incipient or actual cardiac failure often describe feelings of ill-defined anxiety or have anxiety dreams that are more related to physical responses than to psychic content. This phenomenon is more easily demonstrated in elderly people in whom arterial changes have resulted in incipient cardiac failure.

Some investigators have held that the birth trauma is the prototype of all anxiety. But the concept of the biological basis for anxiety does not invalidate the possibility that the experience of birth is significant in terms of later anxiety. The nature of its effect has to be reevaluated.

Phyllis Greenacre has studied the significance of the birth trauma from a somewhat modified approach.[1] She accepts Freud's concept that anxiety originally occurs only when sensory stimulation exceeds the potential for motor discharge. If motor discharge is not possible or is inadequate, anxiety results. This concept is not too different from the one stated above—that fear or anxiety occurs only when a situation that is potentially dangerous or is anticipated to be dangerous cannot be mastered.

According to the authorities quoted by Greenacre, intrauterine fetal development is such that the development of motor activity precedes that of sensory response. Thus, under the ordinary conditions of normal pregnancy, there is always an adequate motor discharge pattern available when sensory stimulation occurs. This ratio, however, is disturbed during the birth process, because motor discharge is restricted during passage through the birth canal, and sensory stimulation is increased over that characteristic of the intrauterine state. Greenacre hypothesizes that if this sensory stimu-

1. Phyllis Greenacre, "The Biological Economy of Birth," in *The Psychoanalytic Study of the Child,* vol. 1 (New York: International Universities Press, 1945), p. 35.

lation is particularly intense—for example, during a long, difficult birth process—biological memory traces may be laid down that remain a part of the basic structure on which the subsequent personality is built. These biological memory traces become roots of a later anxiety pattern. She suggests that it is equally possible that a similar imbalance between sensory stimulation and motor discharge may occur during intrauterine life.[2]

Certain infants appear to be more sensitive to stimuli than others. This fact is observed after the first few days following birth, perhaps after a shorter or longer period of a type of sleep that may be more related to sensory exhaustion than to the normal sleep of the neonate. Furthermore, in the study of certain children one observes a behavior picture that suggests a diffusely anxious child, but no content is elicited that would warrant the anxiety. The parents report that this child has always been "nervous." Often by the time such children are seen by a diagnostician, the superficial picture is one of excessive activity—jerky movements, poor coordination which appears to be based more on their eagerness to perform than on inherently poor coordination due to organic limitations, and an inability to sit still or, as the teacher reports, to concentrate. Observing the child, one senses that all this activity may be an attempt to master an overwhelming anxiety. In some cases of this kind, certain origins of the anxiety may be revealed after careful exploration. The behavior picture, although it becomes less dramatic with therapy, does not change except in degree. During intrauterine life or at birth these children may have been overwhelmed by stimuli that could not be discharged and, therefore, biological memory traces were laid down that remain the root of later anxiety. As later forms of anxiety take shape, they appear as intense as they are not only because of the anxiety-producing situation but because a stimulus is experienced by a trigger-sensitive organism.

Greenacre considers the state of the newborn that is suggestive of an anxiety pattern as indicative of a "preanxiety state." She says, "While anxiety as such cannot exist until there is some dawning ego sense and therefore some individual psychological content, the forerunner of anxiety exists in a condition of irritable responsiveness of the organism, at first appearing in a number of loosely organized reflex responses."[3] At present it is difficult to state definitively

2. *Ibid,* p. 34.
3. *Ibid.,* p. 48.

whether this type of trigger anxiety is due to intrauterine experiences, to birth experiences at which time memory traces were laid down, or to a brain injury at birth which produced a more reactive nervous system. There could also be a constitutional factor that is as yet not clear. A great deal more research is needed before any but speculative conclusions can be reached.

Survival Anxiety

Another early manifestation of anxiety, "survival anxiety," is a familiar experience to everyone. It plays an important part in the continuity of life, triggering self-protective mechanisms that defend the individual from destruction. This response may be excessive, however, and with psychic development may become part of a broader anxiety response. Certain children do not quite fit the picture Greenacre describes.[4] They are not in a state of reactive alertness so much as they are apprehensive about the possibility of impending catastrophes. Their conceptualization of the world is one in which disastrous surprises are always potentially in the offing and they struggle to be prepared or to avoid these ill-defined dangers. It has been suggested that the initial psychological trauma resulting in such attitudes occurred during the neonatal period when the child is considered as responding at the primary functional level of development. It is at that time that the survival urge exists in its most primitive biological form. It is also during that time that the infant may be exposed to experiences of deprivation that may actually threaten survival. Those experiences are not necessarily related to deprivation of food or exposure to direct physical trauma but rather to the deprivations of other gratifications that are important. Later, the clinical picture presented suggests that patterns developed during that early biological state, with the development of affective response, become anxiety. The individual always feels threatened by impending catastrophe, and there is no defense against its occurrence except his own efforts. He cannot depend on others because they are either unwilling or unable to function effectively. This individual, then, suffers from chronic anxiety.

4. See, Phyllis Greenacre, *Trauma, Growth and Personality* (New York: W. W. Norton, 1952).

Four Types of Anxiety

Anna Freud identifies four kinds of anxiety against which the individual strives to defend himself: (1) superego anxiety, (2) objective anxiety, (3) instinctual anxiety, and (4) anxiety created by the threatened disruption of synthesis.[5] Superego anxiety is the easiest to define. It is a response to the threat that an instinctual drive will find expression in a form unacceptable to the superego. It is preceded by objective anxiety, the fear of the outside world as a source of punishment. The attempt to protect the self from anxiety is one of the nuclear factors in the formation of the neuroses. It would appear that educational methods might be developed that would direct the discharge of destructive, aggressive impulses so that those impulses would not be turned against the self with the resultant too punitive superego. If punishment could be deleted from patterns of child rearing so that objective anxiety would not be experienced, neurosis-producing anxiety could be avoided. In answer to this suggestion for prophylaxis against the neuroses through radical modification of child rearing, Anna Freud states, "Psychoanalytic experience destroys the prospect of an effective prophylaxis. The human ego, by its very nature, is never a promising soil for the unhampered gratification of instinct."[6]

What the danger is that arouses the anxiety created by the threatened discharge of an instinctual urge is more difficult to define. Anna Freud suggests that the anxiety created by the threatened disruption of synthesis of conflicting impulses is, like superego anxiety, a developmental phenomenon. This view reflects an early concept of ego development; integration and adaptation were seen as two of the chief components of ego functioning, and the ego was considered to become functional with the development of the reality sense. As indicated in Chapter 6, the author considers adaptation-integration an inherent drive, manifested differently as a result of the complexity of the tasks that increase with maturation. If one observes children exposed to multiple stimuli, all of which are so intense that none can be ignored effectively, one notes that the resulting tension often carries with it an affect suggestive of anxiety.

5. Anna Freud, *The Ego and the Mechanisms of Defense,* vol. 2 (New York: International Universities Press, 1966), pp. 54–61.
6. *Ibid.,* pp. 58–59.

Anxiety dreams of explosions, while uninterpretable except in the context of the particular patient's material, are in some instances indicative of the source of the anxiety state, a fear that everything will disintegrate.

Treatment Considerations

As has been stated earlier, in any area of psychological study, to fractionate for microscopic study is to lose the significance of the whole, unless each fraction is later related to that whole. Thus, only under a psychological microscope can anxiety be divided as it has been in the previous material. Other divisions of anxiety, based upon its source, could undoubtedly be made with equal or more validity. Anxiety is a response to anticipated danger that cannot be, or it is anticipated cannot be, mastered. If Greenacre's concept of "basic anxiety" proves to be valid, such anxiety is present in everyone, with its intensity dependent on the degree of intrauterine and birth trauma experienced by the individual. It is on this "basic anxiety" or, if one does not accept Greenacre's concept, on the biological response of alertness to danger that all later anxiety grows.

A differentiation of the dominant factor in anxiety has some significance for the choice of therapeutic techniques. Greenacre's "basic anxiety" cannot be resolved by analytic therapy. Equally so the "survival anxiety" discussed above (which is actually a part of Greenacre's conceptualization related to the precognitive stage of infant development and, in that sense, "preanxiety") is not effectively relieved by therapy. It should also be pointed out that these responses are not truly neurotic forms of anxiety. They persist on a biological level, stimulating thought content but not being based on thought content. However, the relief of the superimposed anxieties that have evolved with development and maturation may result in minimal evidence of suffering or of affect from the "basic anxiety."

Anna Freud points out that superego anxiety is the most amenable to therapy because its source is within the individual. In the therapy of children, objective anxiety can be decreased by parent education if that education is effective. Disintegrative anxiety can be relieved by decreasing the stimuli, by strengthening the integrative and adaptive patterns of the individual through clarifying what is pressing for integration or demanding adaptive responses, and by "educational" support in dealing with multiple stimuli. She indicates that instinctual anxiety is the most difficult kind to relieve wisely, because destruction of the barriers against free instinctual discharge can be dangerous unless the discharge can be channeled constructively.

The psychologically healthy individual handles fear and anxiety aroused by realistic dangers by the utilization of any realistic, protective measures that are available to him. Neurotic anxiety is dealt with by the utilization of the psychological defense mechanisms. "Basic anxiety" or "biological preanxiety" cannot be dealt with, but it causes a state of chronic alertness which may lead to over-protectiveness against real dangers and to reinforcement of the neurotic defenses.

[17]

Mechanisms of
Adaptation and Defense

As was pointed out earlier, one of the functions of the ego is to make possible the discharge of internal impulses and the gratification of internal needs in a form acceptable to the superego and within the framework of the demands of the individual's reality world. When this integration is successful, the result is an adaptive pattern of behavior. But when the ego fails to achieve such an adaptive pattern, defense mechanisms are utilized to allay the anxiety created by the incompatibility of the forces impinging on it.

This description of the distinction between adaptive and defensive mechanisms is only relatively valid. It can be criticized on the basis that the ego utilizes defense mechanisms for the sake of adaptation; therefore, defense mechanisms are in themselves adaptive. Justification for making a differentiation lies in clinical considerations. Certain behavior patterns serve the individual adaptively without requiring the expenditure of psychic energy in excess of that inherent in the behavioral task itself. In contrast, other behavior patterns do require the excessive expenditure of energy in order to prevent a disruption of the behavioral pattern and thus a chaotic, anxiety-producing state. For example, a man who has been seriously crippled from birth possesses an adequate intellectual endowment. During the course of his development he learns to express through his intellectual activity many internal urges that might be expressed by others through motor activity. This is an adaptive pattern. Another individual may similarly express most of his internal impulses through intellectual activity, but he does so because of the neurotic inhibition of an urge to express those impulses motorially. In the latter instance, the man's intellectual activity is the result of the ego's defense against the discharge of those impulses through unacceptable channels. In turn, the need to prevent the utilization of unacceptable channels necessitates the expenditure of psychic energy in excess of that required for the intellectual activity itself.

165

This example points out another aspect of adaptive and defensive behavior. The tools employed by the ego are the same in both cases. It is the function they serve, whether they are enabling or blocking, that determines whether they are adaptative or defensive mechanisms. This differentiation will become clearer as the specific psychic tools utilized by the ego are discussed. In general, adaptive mechanisms enrich the personality; defense mechanisms cripple it. Heinz Hartmann makes a comparable differentiation of the defenses but on a different basis. He introduced the concept of "secondary autonomy of the ego,"[1] and, in accordance with this concept, certain defenses are first utilized in conflictual situations. Once the conflictual situation is resolved through the utilization of certain defense mechanisms, however, conflict is no longer manifested in each related situation; the defense mechanism originally utilized then becomes an automatic response and an inherent part of the individual's behavior patterns and personality. For example, toilet training in our culture creates a conflict between the wish to smear or soil and the wish to retain and enlarge parental love. This conflict is finally resolved in neatness; the soiling impulse is directed toward destroying dirt rather than creating it, and thus reversal serves the wish to preserve the love of the parents. Neatness finally becomes a part of the modus operandi of the individual; it is no longer the direct expression of a conflict but an autonomous response. This concept allows for the human race to be civilized without the assumption being necessarily justified that civilization is only built on a squirming mass of instinctual impulses that, for example, threaten at each sight of a piece of dust to press for the release of anal impulses to smear all clean surfaces. It also implies that a man can save his father from an oncoming, speeding car without evidencing a defense against his death wishes for his father. That the defenses against the basic conflicts created by the primitive drives sustain their repression, or in other ways avoid their direct discharge, is not contradicted by this concept. The only implication is that the utilization of the defense to avoid or resolve a conflict is the original source of the defense, but is only one aspect of its function. The other aspect of its function is not directly related to a threatened, direct expression of those impulses. Rather it is an autonomous ego response, related to adaptation, and it is a tool of a broader conflict-free area of ego functioning.

1. Heinz Hartmann, *Ego Psychology and the Problem of Adaptation* (New York: International Universities Press, 1958), p. 26.

Anna Freud refers to sublimation as an ego defense but indicates that, in contrast to the other defenses, it relates to the "study of the normal rather than to that of the neuroses," being as it is a displacement of instinctual aims. This statement suggests that sublimation, as she defines it, is related to the above concept of adaptive patterns of behavior.[2]

Otto Fenichel approaches the question of the adaptive-defensive system in a somewhat different way. He defines sublimation as a "successful defense," the others as pathological defenses. He states, "Conflicts between instinctual demands and fear of guilt feelings are not necessarily pathological. The way in which conflicts are handled determines whether or not the further course is a normal or a pathological one."[3] He indicates, for example, that "Certain disgust reactions—usual among civilized people—that show no trace of infantile instinctual tendencies against which they were originally developed are successful defenses and thus can be grouped under the general heading of sublimation." He points out that sublimation "does not designate a specific mechanism; various mechanisms may be present in successful defenses such as a change from passivity to activity, a turning around upon the subject, a reversal of aims into its object. The common factor is that under the influence of the ego, aim or object, or both, is changed without blocking an adequate discharge . . . sublimated impulses find their outlet though drained via an artificial route; whereas others do not."[4] In this sense sublimation is synonymous with "adaptation" as used in the preceding discussion.

The distinction between adaptive and defensive mechanisms implies, however, a different philosophical approach to personality development than that implied in the concept of successful and pathogenic defenses. In the latter concept the perhaps invalid inference can be drawn that a value judgement is involved which states, in effect, that the organism is born bad and becomes good by partial destruction of the self or conversion of the self into something different. This inference is certainly drawn when humor becomes a means of allaying social anxiety. It has become a worn-out joke that when a person says, "I hope you are feeling better," he is disguising

2. Anna Freud, *The Ego and the Mechanisms of Defense* (New York: International Universities Press), p. 52.
3. Otto Fenichel, *The Psychoanalytic Theory of Neurosis* (New York: W. W. Norton, 1945).
4. *Ibid.* See also Chapter 9 of Fenichel for further clarification.

his wish that you had died. This conceptualization of the psychic structure is also reflected in the use of the term aggression as synonymous with hostility.

In stressing the ego adaptive tools as a means of expression rather than suppression, a different concept of the primitive psychic structure becomes possible. It is certainly true that primitive impulses are incompatible if expressed in their primary form. This does not imply that they are inherently bad but rather that they can be bad for each other. They need not be, if they can be discharged through channels that do not interfere with each other. Such patterns of discharge lead to integration of the multiple impulses. (Although the factor of the demands of reality has been referred to frequently in this material, this factor is considered in this text as significant in terms of the instinctual alloplastic drive as discussed in Chapter 6 on inherent needs and drives.) Neurotic defenses develop only when adaptive patterns fail. Socialization thus is the end result of the adaptive discharge of inherent impulses, not the result of distortion or inhibition of inherent impulses. If too broad distortion or inhibition of inherent drives occurs, socialization does not result. Every individual utilizes certain neurotic defenses; it is their relative extent as compared to adaptive patterns that determines the individual's relative psychological illness or health.

Origin of Defense Mechanisms

Why have the defense mechanisms originated in the form they have? Attempts have been made by several writers to trace their origin and the developmental stage at which they appear. Anna Freud concluded that much more would have to be known about their early manifestations before any definitive answer could be given to the question.[5] The following concepts are tentative and represent speculations rather than confirmed conclusions.

Is it possible that the defense mechanisms are exaggerations of the adaptive mechanisms, the latter being the earlier structure? (Neither can occur without some kind of conflict.) Can it be that when the adaptive mechanisms threaten to fail, the same mechanisms, or others that have proved effective in the past, are more intensely utilized and become neurotic defenses, thus crippling rather than enriching the personality? For example, when primitive man discovered that by hiding in a cave and barricading the entrance so that the

5. Freud, *The Ego and the Mechanisms of Defense.*

wild animals that threatened his existence could not enter, he was using a means of adaptation to his environment. He was physically defending himself against outside attack, not against instinctual impulses. This mode of self-protection was effective and thus became a part of his way of life. He also found that a club, a sharpened stone, or an available tree served to protect him when he ventured forth for food. He did not, therefore, confine himself to permanently hiding in the cave. However, another caveman feared that other adaptive tools would not function beyond the confines of the cave. He thus barricaded himself in it and would not venture forth. An adaptive mechanism had become a neurotic defense, and ultimately it would become the source of his destruction rather than his survival.

If further study of adaptive behavior and thus of psychological health should indicate that there are chronologically earlier manifestations of adaptive response, the defenses would then originate, under certain conditions, from the development of the adaptive mechanisms. Although parallel circumstances never justify the arbitrary assumption of parallel functioning, an assumption of contrast in functioning should be carefully scrutinized. In the physical organism there are aspects of coordination for adequate function that become exaggerated only under a strain. The formation of scar tissue is a mode of body defense that is an exaggeration of normal adaptive functioning. Scars develop when an injury to the skin is sufficient to necessitate the excessive mobilization of adaptive tools to enable some form of healing to occur.

Perhaps there are clues to the roots from which adaptive patterns grow to become, under unusual strain, neurotic defenses. In order to explore this possibility it is most challenging to consider the specific defense mechanisms Anna Freud has listed,[6] although a perusal of the literature will indicate that the definition of these defenses becomes increasingly confusing the more one studies the expansion of the concepts she originally presented. In the present discussion no attempt will be made to clarify the terminology in terms of other discussions. The intent is to define defense mechanisms descriptively

Regression

Regression may occur when an individual is confronted with a psychological task that is too difficult for him to master, or with a conflict he cannot resolve. He then regresses to a level of development at which he had more adequately achieved a resolution of his conflict, or to a level at which his gratification was more readily attained. With regression he may again manifest the conflicts of the earlier period and reexperience their mastery. Because of the pressure of his additional problems, he may now be unable to master those earlier conflicts as he did formerly and therefore will utilize his old defenses with gréater force, or he may utilize the defense mechanisms of the past for handling the new task. In the psychopathology of adult life this can be illustrated in the development of a phobic state in response to the arousal of sexual impulses prohibited because of the ineffectively resolved oedipal conflict. The phobic state becomes contaminated by compulsive hand-washing. The individual, unable to defend himself effectively against the sexual impulses by accepting the limits imposed by the phobia, regresses to the anal state of development. But now the psyche is absorbed not only with the characteristically anal struggle with cleanliness but with the prohibited sexuality, which is dirty and must be washed off. The sexual guilt in such cases is frequently associated with guilt over impulses of either an autoerotic or a mutual masturbatory nature.

Regression is frequently observed in children when they are faced with demands for adaptation that they cannot meet. A familiar example is that of a child who, during the early phase of the oedipal period, is faced with the problems created by the arrival of a new sibling. He may begin to soil, show marked ambivalence toward his loved objects, and become increasingly negativistic. His behavior at this time may reach an intensity that is a caricature of that of the two-year-old, an intensity that was not true of his handling of the original experiences with the conflict of the anal period. The advent of the new baby has resulted in a regression to an earlier level of development. Because he has to deal not only with the oedipal conflicts and the resultant anxiety but also with the introduction of an additional rival, his tenuous ego maturation collapses. This response is not a true defense mechanism that protects the ego but is an evidence of ego failure.

This type of regression points out a characteristic of regression that raises an important question. When regression is manifested in this form, its potential for protecting the ego is not readily discernible. This regression does, however, serve the ego inasmuch as it temporarily decreases the pressure that has mounted with the onset of the oedipal phase thereby permitting the remobilization of adap-

6. *Ibid.*

tive strengths. However, this remobilization is possible only if the environment is tolerant of the regressive manifestations. At this time in the child's life, if the environment is not tolerant, typical anal defenses may take over to master both the oedipal conflicts and the reactivated anal conflicts and to determine the development of an anal character pattern in the future adult personality.

Regressive solution of the oedipal-sibling struggle may prove to have a more easily recognized defensive value. In regressing to the anal level, the child may find erotic gratification in his negativism, his soiling, and the punishment that results from that behavior. This gratification serves as a substitute for the phallic gratification he seeks but fears and may become the beginning of masochism. Moreover, regression from the oedipal period to the ambivalence of the anal period can result in the erotic goals of the latter period finding substitute gratification in the hostile attacking phase of the ambivalence and thus reinforce any sadistic aspects of the earlier phase.

Repression and Denial

Repression as a defense mechanism causes impulses, experiences, or affects to be excluded from consciousness. Its potential function is to protect the ego from being flooded by the instinctual impulses of the id, from experiences that would arouse instinctive, objective, or superego anxiety, and from affects that would overwhelm it. Repression in actuality may be a specific form of regression; its aim is to permit regression to the stimulus-free state of the sleeping neonate. This formulation implies that the unconscious has, in part, the function of attempting to recreate the tension-free nirvana that would appear to be the state of the neonate when neither stimulus-hungry nor nutrition-hungry.

Repression is also an adaptive mechanism. It prevents internal stimuli from coming to consciousness and, through the comparable mechanism of denial, the impact of external stimuli is avoided. If one is concentrating while reading a difficult book, the reader does not respond to other stimuli. If someone comes into the room and makes a request, the reader does not consciously hear the words, although he may respond. Never having become a part of consciousness the request is "forgotten" or not heard. Many of the stimuli that result in the defensive use of repression are never conscious. In the latter example, however, the repression and denial mechanism serve as neurotic defenses. In the former case the same mechanisms are adaptive. The primary task is to achieve an understanding of the book, and other responses are repressed or denied before they become conscious. This may have its anlage in such obvious behavior as the neonate's closing his eyes when exposed to too bright a light, or the loss of hunger sensations in extreme starvation.

The adaptive function of repression and denial becomes a defense mechanism when massive, instinctual discharge or extensive, external stimuli having neurotic significance threaten ego integration.

Projection and Introjection

Projection and introjection as defense mechanisms are opposing types of response but both serve defensive functions. In projection, ideas and affects that are unacceptable are attributed to others and denied as part of the self. As a defense the individual denies a part of himself and distorts the object on which he projects his unacceptable ideas or affects. In extreme form this is an aspect of paranoia. Introjection takes on the self the characteristics of another by identification.

The concept of introjection has resulted in many divergent theories. Introjection has been described as an actual taking in of an object. The earliest occurrence, according to this conceptualization, is during nursing when the source of food is cannibalistically taken into the self. This impulse, motivated by the pleasure experienced from the food and thus a wish to incorporate (swallow) its source, is also seen as destroying that which is taken in. Thus, introjection becomes a destructive force. Fenichel, in discussing this defense mechanism, writes, "Originally the idea of swallowing an object is an expression of affirmation, as such it is the prototype of instinctual satisfaction, not of a defense against instincts. At the stage of the purified pleasure ego, everything pleasant is introjected. In the last analysis all sexual aims are derivatives of incorporation aims. Simultaneously, introjection is a prototype of regaining the omnipotence previously projected onto adults. Incorporation, however, although an expression of 'love' objectively destroys the object as an independent thing in the external world. Upon becoming aware of this fact, the ego learns to use introjection for hostile purposes as an executive of destructive impulses and also as a model for the definite defense mechanism."[7]

7. Fenichel, *The Psychoanalytic Theory of Neurosis*, p. 147.

The concept of identification rather than cannibalistic incorporation as a synonym of introjection seems more plausible. As a defense mechanism introjection would appear to be identification with the person who is the source of the conflict. With introjection the self concept is distorted and the self is seen not as a self but as an external object. The use of identification as a defense is apparent during the oedipal period in which the child identifies with the powerful parent and incorporates into his own superego the punitive attitude of the parent. This identification with the punitive parent, however, is a neurotic defense only when the parent is so feared that a rigid, over-severe superego develops, and when instinctual urges must be repressed so early and completely that little or no opportunity is available for alternate paths of discharge.

The earliest manifestation of projection and introjection occurs perhaps as the result of the gradual establishment of the self as separate from the object; the potential for both projection and introjection stems from the early symbiotic relationship in which the infant is one with the mother. Both projection and introjection thus reestablish the oneness, but reality awareness maintains the separateness. Thus, instead of the self and object becoming one, attitudes, feelings, and behavior are displaced from the self to the object or from the object to the self. Projection and introjection as adaptive tools are illustrated in the development of a healthy ego ideal and a superego: A healthy ego ideal and a healthy superego permit adequate discharge for instinctual impulses, either directly as in sexual orgasm or indirectly as in creativeness, constructive ambition, and other typical behavior patterns of relatively mature adults. Their use in adaptation is demonstrable in altruism, in empathy, and in other personality characteristics that lead to gratification of many instinctual impulses through relatedness to others rather than through relatedness only to the self. Only when they fail as means of adaptation are they utilized as neurotic defenses. When this occurs in the more extreme form, paranoid ideas are expressed; the image of the self becomes vague or disappears or the outline of the objective disappears, the self and the object becoming interchangeable or the one being replaced by the other.

Reaction Formation

Reaction formation is the psychological phenomenon in which, as Fenichel states, there are "cramped and rigid attitudes, hindering the expression of contrary impulses." Fenichel would limit the use of the term to those examples in which the reaction formation avoids secondary repression by making a "once and for all" definitive change of the personality. An everyday example of this is the individual who radiates "sweetness and light" under all circumstances if possible, but who reveals the previously hidden hostility when under stress or in indirect, disguised ways. Reaction formation responses can be traced at least as far back as the anal period in normal development. The toilet training experience becomes a factor in the development of neatness; the child identifies with the parents' disapproval of soiling and renounces his soiling impulses. In doing so he assumes an attitude of dislike of soiling and enjoyment of neatness. If his impulse to soil is very strong, the attitude of the external world and finally his own attitude are very repressive. The reaction formation may then be utilized as a neurotic defense and compulsive neatness may result.

Although it appears that reaction formation has its origin in the anal period it may, like any defense pattern, be utilized against impulses of the oral period. For example, a person who dislikes eating may be experiencing that revulsion as a defense against oral impulses striving for expression. A person may refuse to eat because of an unconscious cannibalistic fantasy that would serve to express hostility. The cannibalistic fantasy could have several derivatives; the object to be eaten could symbolically represent the hated person. To avoid this symbolic acting out of the hostility, eating is inhibited.

Reaction formation is not always a neurotic defense; again it may be an adaptive pattern. For example, if neatness is comfortably maintained, it permits the gratification of other impulses. It is rewarded by approval and evidence of affection from parental figures. It does not, however, inhibit all discharge of the impulse to soil. Soiling is permitted within certain limits. The artist can paint; the housemaker can bake a cake; the businessman or woman can enjoy working in their gardens. As another example, the capacity to react pleasantly in a potentially unpleasant situation is a reaction formation that is the key characteristic of diplomacy. Such a response may be consciously chosen or it may be so much a part of the personality it has become automatic.

Reversal

The adaptive, potentially defensive, mechanism of reversal probably also has its inception during the anal period. Whereas reaction formation is a response against an instinctual drive, reversal is a response against a threat from the external world. The toddler's feeling of inadequacy when faced with the powerful adults in his environment reverses the situation; he attempts to be the immovable object, hoping the force will prove to be resistible. Reality-determined anxieties may be handled by a reversal mechanism. For example, during a storm a small child, obviously frightened by flashes of lightning, was apparently conceptualizing for the first time. He watched tensely for each recurrence and became progressively more anxious. After one flash he exclaimed, "Pretty, pretty." His anxiety apparently decreased but the tension remained. He seemed to be eagerly anticipating the next flash, greeting each with "Pretty, pretty." As the storm subsided, he began to cry, asking for more. His disappointment appeared to be genuine. The use of the word "pretty" seemed to be particularly significant because it was a word he used with discrimination, applying it to objects which he enjoyed.

As a defense mechanism, reversal can result in the individual's acting as if the reverse of reality were true. Probably certain pathological liars actually do not "lie"; they reverse reality, believe the reversal, and report only what they believe to be true.

Isolation

Isolation as a neurotic defense serves to separate the affect from its source. The experience is accepted and remains conscious but the affect is absent. It is possible that the affect is discharged in seemingly unrelated situations. Isolation as a neurotic defense is readily demonstrated in compulsive neurosis. The small child learns to isolate events from their affective significance. If his toy is broken by a playmate, his response is likely to be an attack on the playmate. Through parental guidance, he comes to accept at least unintentional breakage with tolerance by checking his affect. He becomes an observer of the event rather than affectively experiencing it.

This capacity to isolate an experience from its affective meaning proves, under certain circumstances, a valuable adaptive tool. It enables an individual to deal realistically with situations of crisis rather than to be overpowered and paralyzed by affect discharge.

Turning Against the Self

The defense of turning against the self is manifested when hostility or other affects are discharged against the self rather than against the object which has been their source. Certain suicidal impulses are examples: the primary murderous impulses are turned against the self and the self is murdered.

It is possible that the mechanism of turning against the self either has its origin at the time of the development of the superego or becomes more frequently utilized at that time. A component of the superego may involve this mechanism. Not only does the child identify with the punitive parent but, in his anger toward the parent which cannot be expressed, he intensifies his own self-punishment by turning his anger against himself. The result may be an excessively punitive superego even though the parent has not been excessively punitive or permissive.

Turning against the self is not always a neurotic defense. Sometimes the behavior of others is understood not by identification but by a critical analysis of the self, in effect turning against the self. It is an adaptive mechanism that enables one to recognize that, in spite of convictions to the contrary, one is not always right. Sometimes it is wise to turn one's feelings about the narcissism of others onto one's own narcissism.

Undoing

Undoing is a defense mechanism frequently observed in obsessive-compulsive neurosis. The individual fantasizes the discharge of an impulse, carries through in fantasy an impulse that is unacceptable or indirectly makes it possible for that impulse to be gratified, then atones for the act or undoes that which would make possible its fulfillment. A boy of twelve who is a compulsive masturbator was convinced that by masturbating once he would somehow destroy his mother. If, however, he masturbated three times in succession, he would save his mother but he himself would die. Very ambivalent toward his mother when angry at her, he masturbated. This meant her destruction which he could not tolerate because of both his guilt and his immature need for her. He then masturbated twice more, which would mean his own destruction and she would be saved. If he masturbated once more, the cycle would be repeated. He would be out of danger but his mother would die.

Such extreme pathology as this boy's is only an exaggeration of a common occurrence. Undoing is not, however, always so dramatic. The young child learns how to undo a misdeed very early, possibly by imitation of the parents. When the child commits a forbidden act, he says he's sorry, sometimes quite spontaneously and without parental demand.

Apologies are always an undoing of an act. The magical implications are accepted by both the apologizer and the person to whom the apology is directed. This is an adaptive way of dealing with human relationships. Only when the act is motivated by unacceptable wishes and therefore must be undone to relieve neurotic stress does this adaptive pattern become a neurotic defense.

A little consideration of the adaptive-defense mechanisms that have been briefly discussed in this chapter will make it clear that this tabulation fractionates the total picture. Fenichel points out that "There are no sharp lines of demarcation between the various forms of defense mechanisms. Reaction formation is related to repression and undoing is related to reaction formation."[8] Rationalization can be discussed as it relates to the denial of emotional needs expressed in behavior. Intellectualization may closely resemble isolation. Whether any of these mechanisms or others are utilized, the question remains whether they are utilized as neurotic defenses or for adaptation. The former represents psychological pathology, the latter, psychological health. As was suggested earlier the former may also be an exaggeration of the latter. Healthy adaptive mechanisms may be the earlier phenomenon rather than the result of the secondary autonomy of the ego. It should be added, however, that some defensive mechanisms may become adaptive mechanisms when the need for the defense is no longer present.

8. *Ibid*, p. 53.

ℒatency Stage

WITH THE PASSING OF THE OEDIPAL stage discussed in Chapter 15, the so-called latency maturational stage evolves. The term "latency" was applied to this stage primarily in relation to the psychosexual aspects of development. Because of the repression of sexual responses to the parent of the opposite sex, infantile sexuality was considered to have come to an end. It was further assumed that all sexuality became dormant from the time of this repression until the resurgence of sexual responses during adolescence. The curiosity characteristic of the oedipal period became desexualized in latency and was the essential stimulus for learning. It was also recognized that not all sexuality was repressed; part of the libidinal drive was sublimated in the gratification of this desexualized curiosity; part of it was sublimated in social relationships with the peer group. And the love for the parent normally did not disappear; only the sexual component was repressed or channeled into other paths for discharge.

There is increasing evidence, however, that this concept of latency is not correct. And the term "latency" is not a satisfactory one to characterize the span of years between the resolution of the oedipal period and adolescence. It is now clear that sexual feelings are not as completely repressed or sublimated as the term implies. Although the sexual feelings toward the parent of the same sex are undoubtedly repressed or redirected, there is not a repression of all sexual feelings. For example, masturbation continues during the latency period, though with less frequency than earlier. Mutual masturbation and mutual exploration between children of the same sex or opposite sexes is not an uncommon occasional occurrence among this age group.

In those instances in which the sexual implications of the oedipal period were never conscious—only derivatives were (which, in the author's opinion, is characteristic of the "normal" oedipal period in our culture)—latency does not represent the result of a repression of sexual feelings. Rather there is continuation of the early repression which was always present and new outlets for the discharge of instinctual urges become available for use.

To return to the original concept of latency, the theory has been that learning becomes possible at this period because energy which primarily was bound to the sexual drive is delibidinalized and becomes available for learning. Similarly, sexual curiosity becomes desexualized and is rechanneled into curiosity about reality. Again, this concept does not reflect the normal patterns of growth. Actually, the rate of learning is most rapid in the first three years of life. Both the child's rate of learning and the intensity of his curiosity actually decreases at about the time of the resolution of the oedipal period. The latency child's learning patterns reflect other aspects of his development more than they do the resolution of the oedipal conflict. This statement is not meant to imply that its resolution is not significant. It only suggests that the learning patterns of the latency child may be determined by many growth factors and, in addition, with the resolution of the oedipal conflict, energy that was previously utilized in handling that conflict is now partially available for learning.

In Chapter 6, it was suggested that there are four inherent drives, but their relationship to the erogenous zones is somewhat ambiguous. In order to understand a concept of latency somewhat different from that usually formulated, this ambiguity must be faced. As has been frequently stressed, any microscopic exploration of the psychic structure tends to destroy the unity of the whole. Yet, integration is a basic need of the living organism. The human psyche cannot be understood by putting the erogenous zones under one microscope and the inherent drives under another. But perhaps, they should be studied equally and separately before they can be recognized as differing aspects of the psyche which are integrated into a common response.

It is conceivable that any instinctual drive may be discharged through a "part of the body" and that the means used is an erogenous zone. Furthermore, the successful discharge of an inherent drive is gratifying per se. Thus the pleasure in the discharge of an instinctual drive and the pleasure derived from the use of the particular part of the body that has become a source of pleasure result in the composite picture of eroticized gratification from the successful attainment of the expression of an instinctual drive.

The Basic Drives in Latency

The fate of the basic drives during latency suggests that latency is not a period of quiescence between the oedipal period and adolescence but rather a period of important growth. The interrelationship of the drives becomes particularly clear at this time.

The libidinal drive has for some time prior to latency found outlet other than the conflictual relationship with the parents. Other child-caring, or simply child-loving people have become important to the child. Now, in latency, the child broadens the scope of his love and spreads it thinner, gradually turning to people outside of his more intimate milieu. He forms new affectional ties, particularly with children of his own age. Although he also turns to other adults, such as teachers, they probably serve primarily in the role of parent surrogates. Gradually, the latency child becomes capable of forming friendships with others and finding gratification from other than family members. If he has gained a sense of security in the past in the intimacy of the family, he faces these broader horizons with confidence and derives greater security from his positive experiences. He also develops increasing tolerance for areas of insecurity because his sources of security have multiplied. Latency is thus the period of socialization in which the child gradually comes to seek love from his fellow man and to give love to his fellow man rather than only seeking love from and giving love to the intimates in his family circle.

During latency the inherent alloplastic drive also results in the child's growing relatedness to others, particularly to his own age group. Curiosity is the intellectual manifestation of this drive. The alloplastic drive is a component of the striving for self-preservation, and curiosity serves to alert a living organism to danger. Moreover, the alloplastic drive becomes the component of curiosity that results in an eagerness to explore. Exploration, however, exposes the individual to uncertainties, unpleasantness, and bafflement. These experiences create tension that can be released only by withdrawal or by mastery. Thus the aggressive drive comes into play to interlock with the alloplastic drive.

Progressively in the life span of the child prior to latency, he not only has developed new ways of exploring the world about him but also has new tools for mastering it. With the beginning of latency there is a coincident development of a capacity to tolerate formal learning. It appears that the aggressive drive now finds expression in part through academic learning. Learning academic material is an active process, a point to be discussed more fully later in this chapter.

Mastery of a new experience or a new idea, however, is not the sole factor in learning. The process of effective learning is dependent on the ability of the person to integrate the facts he learns—an expression of the integrative-adaptive drive. To give a simple example, the child learns what an apple is, what an orange is, and what fruit is. He also learns that two plus two are four. Two apples plus two oranges do not make four apples or four oranges; it makes four pieces of fruit. A variety of known facts are integrated in the final answer. The process of learning, including the learning of the most complicated scientific and philosophical truths, is based on the same ability to integrate isolated facts or concepts that have been mastered.

It should be borne in mind that it is not only in academic work that the alloplastic, aggressive, and integrative drives fuse. And it is not only in latency that their integration occurs. Their progressive fusion and integration goes on from the time the psyche and soma become functionally differentiated and continue until deterioration lessens the energy available for the drives. By the time the child attains the maturation of the latency period, however, he has a wealth of means by which to find new things to integrate and a wealth of tools to expedite that integration.

Reality Orientation

During early latency, conflicts inherent in the maturational pattern prior to this age have reached some solution. The psychic energy thus freed can now be utilized in other psychological activities. Many of the adaptive patterns have become sufficiently established so that they function effectively and permit many impulses to find channels of discharge. The superego and ego ideal have become sufficiently a part of the child's personality and character structure so that his behavior is relatively compatible with both.

The latency child is primarily oriented to reality and the real world. Much of his time and thought are spent in solving the problems the external world presents to him. His emotional life tends to be geared to the external events he experiences; he is happy when events are enjoyable and angry when external events frustrate him. When external events are frustrating or the source of unhappiness, he gradually comes to deal with them factually and to adapt to their reality. This mode of adaptation is often strikingly demonstrated in the response of a child of nine or so to the death of a significant person. At this age, the child does not have a prolonged grief period; he may cry and be sad for a day or so but rapidly wants to separate himself from others who are grieving and to return to school and normal play activities. This response is frequently misinterpreted as evidence that the child does "not care." Analysis of adults who lost a parent during this period does not warrant such a conclusion. The child does care and does experience grief. But the discomfort of grief is avoided by the defense of activity. To him death becomes a fact; it is not allowed to be experienced with prolonged emotional turmoil. The child's reality adaptation then becomes a defense mechanism.

Needs and Capacities

The latency child is able to accept reasonable demands from the adults with whom he has contact and to accept the restrictions placed by society on his impulses. If he has an opportunity for satisfactory social contacts, if the demands made on him at school are within his intellectual capacity, if the restrictions upon his behavior are reasonably geared to his capacity to tolerate frustration and to renounce his impulses, and if the total environment balances demands and frustrations with reasonable gratifications and recognition, he presents relatively few problems to his parents or to society. On the other hand, if these optimum conditions are not present or if he has not resolved his earlier conflicts satisfactorily, he may give evidence— often for the first time—of more or less serious maladjustment.

Some of the difficulties of this age group are because of the failure of the parents, the school, or the community to recognize the child's needs and capacities as well as the limitation in his capacities. The child, now that he is in school and is freer in the environment, is too often expected to act as an adult. He is suddenly expected to be able, for six hours of the day, to control his behavior in order to conform to the school situation. He must arrive at school on time, properly dressed and properly fed. He must sit quietly for three consecutive hours or be active, according to the dictates of the teacher. This period may be broken by a short recess when he is supposed to be able to make a complete social adjustment to a group of confused children of his own age. Six hours of the child's time are therefore occupied by regimented activities, a regimentation that is foreign to his past experiences. The physician decrees that the growing child should have at least ten hours of sleep at night. This theoretically allows eight hours of freedom for the child. Often, however, parents decide the child should have music or dancing lessons, should practice certain hours, or should study a school subject in which he is slow. Certainly, says the parent, he should develop some sense of responsibility and learn to help maintain the home he enjoys. So little domestic tasks come into the picture. The average child, doing well in school and meeting the demands of the classroom and his social group, is in reality manifesting a surprising sense of responsibility. Tremendous respect is due the child who meets the demands society places upon him during the latency period. On the whole he does better than the adults around him.

Adults rarely give proper credit to the child for his adaptability. The responsibility he assumes is taken for granted. If the increased demands made of him finally exceed his ability, he is considered, if not a problem child, at least a child with problems. He reacts to the unreasonable demands by becoming irritable, defiant, and tearful.

The serious problems of this age group, however, are the problems that result from the failures of earlier childhood. If the child has not had adequate emotional security during the previous stages of development, or if his relationship with his parents has been such as to necessitate a distortion of the healthy emotional growth process, the effect may be evident in the poor adjustment the child makes in latency. The symptoms are multiple and the causes of any symptom may also be multiple.

Motivations of Delinquent Behavior

Delinquency, from a structural point of view, presupposes a weak, absent, or distorted superego. A healthy, strong superego will not permit flagrantly asocial behavior such as stealing, one of the common misdemeanors of childhood. Certain children, however, will steal because of a distorted superego. Bound by a powerful but unconscious sense of guilt, the child feels a need to be punished and thus to make retribution for a "crime," the nature of which is not conscious. If punishment is obtained, the guilt will be relieved. Unable to seek punishment for the primary crime, because its nature is unkown to him, he commits an actual misdeed in order to be punished. In committing the delinquent act, be it stealing or any other type of asocial behavior, he does it in a manner that makes detection inevitable. His clumsiness belies his assumed clever misdemeanor or crime. He is caught and punished. If institutionalized he is often the ideal inmate, conforming because he is actually grateful to the administration for the relief from guilt offered by the punishing situation. Released from the institution, he reverts to his former behavior pattern. He again becomes delinquent. His guilt has not been relieved permanently because the unconscious crime still exists.

Sometimes the child seeking punishment does not conform well in a correctional institution, regardless of its type. In certain cases, if those in charge of the child are cruel, he will behave in a way that invites punishment. If the institution is "modern" and offers a minimum of punishment, the child will do everything to provoke what punishment does exist. He will often present a picture of an extremely frustrated child because of the need for punishment that he feels is not being adequately met.

Stealing may also be an expression of a wish to obtain love and security, which undoubtedly has a bearing on the sociological findings of high delinquency in low economic groups. In families where bare necessities are uncertain and are secured only with a great effort, an atmosphere of anxiety inevitably prevails. Material things are then important factors in establishing a sense of security. A feeling of security derives not only from love but also from freedom from cold and starvation. The child under marginal economic conditions learns early that material things are a source of security. Frightened by the economic insecurity of his parents, and by the deeper insecurity he feels in his affectional relationship with worried, tense parents, he may steal material things in a symbolic attempt to steal security.

The symbolic aspect of the mechanism is clearer in the stealing observed in certain children of a higher economic group. With money in their pockets and the assurance of availability of more when it is needed, these children will steal a comic book, a trinket from the ten-cent store, a toy of which there is a duplicate at home. Even with money in his pocket, the child avoids the obligation to pay. He refuses to give love by stealing a material symbol of love. It never satisfies, and so the stealing becomes compulsive. Many of these children steal money from their parents. Wanting love from the parents and unable to obtain it, they steal what seems to be the equivalent—money. This may occur even when the parents are generous in giving money. If money is all they can give, the child steals more in an attempt to satisfy his yearning for a really meaningful gift from the parent.

Stealing may also be an expression of hostility toward the parents or toward society generally. In the prohibition placed on taking from others the child senses the implication that those objects are of value to the possessor. He can thereby attack the individual by taking away a prized possession.

Sometimes children steal money for very practical reasons. They want the money in order to buy candy and other gifts to give to children by whom they would like to feel accepted but with whom they feel insecure. The child who feels economically and socially inferior to his playmates is prone to utilize this mechanism for solving his feeling of insecurity. Feeling insecure in his more significant relationship, he attributes this insecurity to the fact that he does not have the money the other children have. He then steals money in order to be able to give the impression of being their equal.

Children who have no tolerance for frustration of their desires may steal because they cannot get what they want in any other way. The absence of the superego control is very apparent in these cases. The child wants what he wants when he wants it and, unable to obtain it by legitimate means, he steals in order to gratify his uncontrollable desires.

Truancy is another example of asocial behavior occurring during the latency period. Like stealing, it also may be related to current situations or may be a symptom of emotional disturbances having their origins in the past. Some children truant from school or run away from home because the situation with which they are faced is untenable. The child's acceptance of school attendance and of returning to his home at prescribed hours indicates how fearful he is of giving up what little security he has and how dangerous the world beyond his immediate environment seems. A child, of course, may run away from home or refuse to attend school because he has the internal strength to escape from a real unpleasantness. The escape may be a means of avoiding punishment for some act he has intentionally or unintentionally committed. It also may be a means of becoming free of a nagging parent or teacher, or it may be a way of avoiding pressure to achieve beyond his capacity. Statistically these cases are probably relatively few in number. Because the average child does not have sufficient confidence in his own ability to cope with the world, most truancy has a deeper significance. This is particularly true when the truancy involves running away from home.

When the truancy has a neurotic basis, several possible explanations must be considered. Some children who have not developed a capacity to enjoy the real world may enjoy their fantasy world more.

This fantasy world may be impinged on by the demands of reality. Running away offers an opportunity for free living out of the fantasy.

Truancy from home with some children has a motivation similar to that of suicide. The child feels unloved at home. He wishes to create guilt in the parents for the way they treat him. He runs away so the parents will worry and therefore feel sorry for what they have done to him. His truancy has an advantage over suicide, because it is possible for him to come back and enjoy the parents' guilt and their retribution. In reality, however, he often returns to punishment. The angry response on the part of the parents increases his feeling of being unloved, which may impel him to run away again with the hope that their guilt may finally be aroused if he stays away longer.

It should be remembered that no type of delinquency has a universal etiology. The preceding discussion of causative factors is not meant to be an exhaustive listing, but is intended only to indicate a few of the types of social and developmental problems which may lead to delinquent behavior.

Establishing Social Relationships

During the latency period children may have difficulty in forming social relationships. Healthy relationships with one's peers require a capacity to accept a loss of identity as an individual and to find gratification in a new identity as part of a group. If the child is unsure of himself as a person in his own right the threat to his own identity is too great. He may withdraw from the group, attempting to maintain his own sense of security by avoiding the hazards of group participation. He may, however, remain in the group, asserting his right to protect himself as a person against the demands of the group. In the most obvious form, this reaction leads to the "bully." Often the "bully" himself has been the victim of domineering parents or siblings so that he has not felt confident of his capacity to defend his own individuality. When placed with children of his own age, who are less powerful people, he recognizes that he has strength to defend himself. He then asserts his power as others have manifested theirs to him and attempts to rule as he has been ruled. The child who is not emotionally secure enough to feel safe as a part of the group may, on superficial observation, give the picture of being a leader. This type of leadership, however, is immature leadership. Closer observation will reveal that the child is leading groups into activity for the sake of his own gratification. True, mature leadership comes only as the child or the adult is able to sense intuitively the desires and goals of the group and is able to fuse them into a common goal that is gratifying to the majority. Such a leader enjoys the activity because of the group, as well as the group because of the activity. The pseudo-leader enjoys only his power over the group.

The roots of the insecurity that results in inadequate social adjustment lie in the prelatency experiences of the child. The child who is insecure in his primary relationship with the parents does not with facility become secure in a group situation. The socially insecure child then needs the protection of adults and greater security with adults before he can make further progress toward adequate socialization. In some instances the early deprivation has been so great that treatment depends on the child's establishing a close relationship with an adult as a substitute parent. No socialization can be expected until the child has received sufficient gratification in a parental relationship. As the child gains the needed security he will often seek broader contacts. If he does not do so, he may need some support from the adult in trying to find his way into a group experience. In other instances of social withdrawal the child needs only a little help in finding himself in the group. This can often be done by leading him into participation in noncompetitive activities where other children are present but where the outcome of the activity is not dependent upon group cooperation. The very presence of other children, however, has value. They prove to be safe companions and therefore can be gradually accepted. As these ties form, the child develops an increased capacity to tolerate a social group and may go from this relatively disorganized group situation into one with a more defined common goal.

It is important to remember that the latency period covers several years, during which time the child is gradually finding his place in a social world. He must be allowed time to evolve and should not be expected to become suddenly a completely adjusted, social human being. A child of six should not be expected to be able to lose himself in identification with the group. A child of twelve, on the other hand, should be able to do so if his development has been healthy. No definite age can be set at which a child should present a picture of rounded social adjustment. The yardstick can only be one of evidence of growth rather than completion of growth. If a child in the course of a year makes progress in his social adjustment, no further treatment is indicated except to protect him as much as is possible from an extremely discouraging failure at his present level or in the next step he takes. If, however, he has made no progress, the reason for his arrest should be studied closely to determine by what means he can be released from whatever is retarding his emotional growth.

School Achievement

One of the school problems of the latency period is emotional blocking in learning. Certain children, in spite of adequate or superior intelligence, fail to learn. This failure may be in all areas of school work or it may be in a specific subject. Reading is the most frequent subject in which blocking occurs. Certain children, who are left-eyed and right-handed, or who are right-eyed and left-handed, may have difficulty learning to read by the method of sight reading. They can, however, learn to read if taught by the phonetic method. If the condition is not recognized and handled early, emotional problems will arise as a consequence that will further hinder the learning process. Repeated failure creates anxiety and lack of confidence and leads to avoidance of tasks that have previously resulted in failure. The child's confidence must be restored before he can be expected to make real progress in the learning process.

In many instances of poor school achievement the emotional problem is more complex and deep-seated. Often the blocking of learning capacities is related to early repression of sexual curiosity. Having asked questions about sex and been censured for his curiosity, or having felt that for some undisclosed reason any questioning about sex was wrong, the child had to deny his interest in learning in that particular area. Normally, sexual curiosity expands to related aspects of life and develops into an eagerness to learn about many things. If the sexual curiosity is repressed before this expansion occurs, the desire to learn is also repressed. Learning in any area is then a forbidden pleasure. In therapy, after these children are able to bring their sexual questions to consciousness and are permitted to satisfy their curiosity, they are able to extend their desire to learn to a wider area. Because reading is a tool for learning they are then free to learn to read.

In other instances reading disabilities are not the result of the child's inhibited sexual curiosity. As stated earlier, learning is an aggressive act. This perhaps is not obvious because superficially learning seems to be a matter of passive reception of facts. This apparent passivity is not real, however. A person takes an active role in learning. The small child, eager to learn, does so with an enthusiasm and zest that can be associated only with an aggressive striving toward gaining a goal. Children who have come to fear their aggressions in the prelatency period will fear the aggressiveness inherent in the learning process. Because learning cannot be absorbed passively, they will be unable to learn.

This concept is substantiated in psychiatric studies of children with reading disabilities. Reading disabilities are much more common with boys than with girls. Because boys are normally more aggressive they are more apt to be submitted to early repressive demands to curb their aggressions. The boy with a reading block is often superficially a very passive child, with evidence of strong aggressions smoldering just below the surface. If he is not overtly passive, his aggressiveness is usually expressed in ways that are immature for his chronological age. In treatment, and without special tutoring, these children will begin to be freer in expressing their aggressions and simultaneously will often begin to read spontaneously. This concept of learning as an aggression, and of a correlation between blocking in learning and the repression of the aggressive drive, does not invalidate the theory of reading difficulties resulting from the repression of sexual curiosity. Striving for sexual information is also an aggressive act. When it is checked, not only the sexual curiosity but also the aggressive strivings are repressed at the same time. Sometimes only those aggressions related to learning have been checked. When the child's sexual curiosity is again brought to consciousness and is accepted, the aggression involved in learning is also released. When, however, all aggression has been repressed, gratification of the sexual curiosity does not suffice. The child, then, must be released from the general inhibition before he is free to learn.

One of the paradoxical situations that lead to much confusion in understanding the motivations behind human behavior is illustrated in the problem of learning and the aggressive drive. Certain individuals, instead of repressing learning because of anxiety over the aggressive implications, use learning as a sublimation for otherwise forbidden aggressiveness. Thus we find the student who, appearing to be a moderately or extremely passive individual, attacks problems of research in science, philosophy, or the arts with a fervor which, if expressed physically, would make him a veritable boxing-ring champion. The teacher, the scholar, or the research man may have found an outlet for aggressions which in their primitive form were unacceptable but which, directed into an academic channel, become a source of gratification to him and a service to humanity. He is the reverse of the child who is unable to learn because of the complete inhibition of his aggressive impulses.

Balancing Freedom and Controls

The nature of the child's relationship to his parents is often revealed for the first time during the latency period. If a child has learned through the intimate day-by-day contact with his parents that adults are accepting, friendly persons, even if at times they impose restrictions, he will turn to new contacts with other adults with the confidence engendered by these early experiences. The confidence may at first be overshadowed by the timidity that is a natural part of an unfamiliar experience. Timidity is often first manifested during the second year of life as the child faces the need to adjust his demands to those of people about him. Timidity may persist well into the latency period. As long as it persists the child is indicating his uncertainty about the new individuals he is called upon to meet. When the child is convinced that other adults are as reliable as his parents, the timidity will disappear. In instances where the parents' unreliability justifies the child's skepticism, the child must first be convinced that other adults are not like his parents before his shyness and uncertainty leave him.

Children often react to other adults in a manner quite different from that which they display toward their parents. Teachers are frequently confused because of the difficulty they may have with a child who, from all reports, has not been a disciplinary problem at home. It is likely that the child has been intimidated by the parents to the point that disobedience is unthinkable. The teacher or other adult seems less formidable. The child then places the resentment he feels toward his parents onto people toward whom he has no hostility and whom he considers less dangerous. Reverse displacement also occurs frequently. As the child enters school he is cognizant of the authority delegated to the teacher; he obeys the school regime without apparent difficulty. At home, however, he becomes defiant and irritable. The pent-up hostility he has felt all day toward the teacher is released on the parents with whom he feels more secure.

The child who fails to develop control of his behavior is a confused and unhappy child. A child is bombarded by many impulses, some of which can be properly gratified with parental approval. Other impulses cannot be easily or completely gratified and the child must develop adequate controls and sublimations. If he is not helped to find a satisfactory balance between control and satisfaction, his behavior becomes random and unpredictable. He is thrashing about for some way to gain gratification and has no pattern to follow. Wise discipline offers the child guidance toward optimum gratification with minimal expenditure of emotional energy in developing suitable controls—giving the child a sense of security and, at the same time, of freedom. The child is aware of limits placed on his behavior which, if accepted by him, assure him of the reward of emotional security. Within these limits the child is free to express himself, gain certain gratifications, and not jeopardize his basic relationships. It assures him that he is protected by those limitations from carrying out impulses which might destroy what he wants to preserve.

It is difficult to define specifically what wise discipline is. Discipline should be geared to the individual child's capacity to tolerate frustration without being overwhelmed by it. When it is not so geared, the child may be "overdisciplined," in which case he may have to become passively accepting of restrictions placed upon impulses that should have some mode of expression. He renounces gratifications instead of finding sublimated outlets for impulses which would be satisfactory both from the standpoint of his own needs and from the standpoint of society. He may, on the other hand, not accept the frustration passively but may refuse to be frustrated, often at the cost of giving up the gratification of being loved. Because the price he must pay for love is too great, he represses his wish to be loved. He then depends on himself for the security he originally sought through the love of others.

Punishment is at times necessary in order to sharpen the necessity for conformity in regard to important issues. There is no "best" form of punishment. Punishment is most meaningful to the child when it is in proportion to the misdemeanor rather than in proportion to the parent's irritation, when it has some relationship to the behavior that necessitates it, and when it is carried out consistently once it is imposed.

Parents, in an attempt to appear reasonable, will on occasion consult the child about the wisdom of some action on the part of the child, intending in the process to have the child agree with the parents. If the child does not agree, the parents then insist that the action still be done in accordance with their judgment. Such parents are intellectually dishonest, and dishonesty of this kind is often confusing to the child. Children should not be offered a choice in conduct unless they are truly free to make the choice. When an issue is at stake in which the parents will accept but one outcome, the ready-made plan should be presented as such. This should not preclude the parents' giving the reasons for the demand; nor should the parents feel any necessity to be defensively prepared for a counterattack. There is no reason for parents to apologize for setting certain requirements for the child to meet as long as the requirements are reasonable and within the child's capacity. Parents with conflict about their own adult status often need to be reassured that they are not only more powerful than the child but that the child looks to them to exercise a protective parental authority.

Parents can impose certain demands and at the same time be generous in allowing the child discretion in making less essential decisions. Most children accept reasonable restrictions if they have the repeated reassuring experience of having their own desires considered when major decisions are not at stake. It is important, however, that the parent's approach to the subject at issue be clearly defined so that the child knows whether the final answer rests with him or with the parent. It is of equal importance that the child not be forced to assume the responsibility of making decisions until he is capable of doing so. Children are as aware as adults are that they do not have the capacity to judge values in an adult world. They are frightened and confused if required to form judgments in matters beyond their ability, but they gain a sense of well-founded confidence if they can be free to make decisions in matters that are a part of a child's world.